MW00650149

FOREWORD

This pamphlet contains the official text of the new Constitution of the State of Montana as adopted by the Constitutional Convention on March 22, 1972 and as ratified by the people on June 6, 1972

The results of the voting on the separately submitted issues concerning the unicameral form of the legislature, gambling and the death penalty have been noted and the directions of the Adoption Schedule have been followed in the printing of the text

The effective date of the Constitution is July 1, 1973, except for sections on annual legislative sessions, reapportionment of the legislature, the size of the legislature and the election and terms of its members (see Sections 1 and 2 of the Transition Schedule, page 44, herein)

Explanatory notes as prepared by the Constitutional Convention and comparing the 1972 sections with the provisions of the Constitution of 1889 are included   The publisher has inserted references to the particular sections of the old Constitution in these Convention Notes

Selected cross-references between sections of the new Constitution and to sections of the Revised Codes of Montana have been added

An Index to the new Constitution begins on page 47

CONSTITUTION OF MONTANA

THE

CONSTITUTION

OF THE

STATE OF MONTANA

AS ADOPTED BY THE CONSTITUTIONAL CONVENTION
MARCH 22, 1972 AND AS RATIFIED BY THE PEOPLE, JUNE 6, 1972

PREAMBLE

We the people of Montana grateful to God for the quiet beauty of our state, the grandeur of our mountains, the vastness of our rolling plains, and desiring to improve the quality of life, equality of opportunity and to secure the blessings of liberty for this and future generations do ordain and establish this constitution

Convention Notes

Preamble is new The old Preamble is
deleted

ARTICLE I
COMPACT WITH THE UNITED STATES

All provisions of the enabling act of Congress (approved February 22, 1889, 25 Stat 676), as amended and of Ordinance No 1, appended to the Constitution of the state of Montana and approved February 22, 1889 including the agreement and declaration that all lands owned or held by any Indian or Indian tribes shall remain under the absolute jurisdiction and control of the congress of the United States, continue in full force and effect until revoked by the consent of the United States and the people of Montana

Convention Notes

Makes it clear that the new constitution does not affect any agreements made with the United States Government when Montana first became a state

ARTICLE II
DECLARATION OF RIGHTS

Section 1 Popular Sovereignty. All political power is vested in and derived from the people All government of right originates with the people, is founded upon their will only, and is instituted solely for the good of the whole

Convention Notes

Identical to 1889 Constitution [Art III, sec 1] Expresses the philosophy that government is founded on the will of the people and is for their good

1

Section 2   Self-government The people have the exclusive right of governing themselves as a free, sovereign, and independent state They may alter or abolish the constitution and form of government whenever they deem it necessary.

Convention Notes

No change except in grammar [Art III, sec 2] Gives Montanans the right to govern themselves and to determine their form of government

Section 3.   Inalienable rights All persons are born free and have certain inalienable rights They include the right to a clean and healthful environment and the rights of pursuing life's basic necessities, enjoying and defending their lives and liberties, acquiring, possessing and protecting property, and seeking their safety, health and happiness in all lawful ways In enjoying these rights, all persons recognize corresponding responsibilities

Compiler s Notes

Section 3 of the Transition Schedule provides that "rights, procedural or substantive, created for the first time by Article II shall be prospective and not retroactive"

Convention Notes

Revises 1889 constitution [Art III, sec 3] by adding three rights, relating to environment, basic necessities, and health The last sentence is also new and provides that in accepting rights people have obligations

Section 4.   Individual dignity. The dignity of the human being is inviolable No person shall be denied the equal protection of the laws Neither the state nor any person, firm corporation, or institution shall discriminate against any person in the exercise of his civil or political rights on account of race, color, sex, culture, social origin or condition, or political or religious ideas

Compiler's Notes

Section 3 of the Transition Schedule provides that "rights, procedural or substantive, created for the first time by Article II shall be prospective and not retroactive."

Convention Notes

New provision prohibiting public and private discrimination in civil and political rights

Cross-References

Freedom from discrimination as civil right, sec 64-301 et seq
Nondiscrimination in education, Const Art X, sec 7

Section 5.   Freedom of religion The state shall make no law respecting an establishment of religion or prohibiting the free exercise thereof.

Convention Notes

Revises 1889 constitution [Art III, sec 4] by using wording of the U S constitution to guarantee free exercise of religion and prohibit the state from establishing a religion

Cross-References

Schools not to instruct in sectarian doctrine, see 75-7521

Section 6   Freedom of assembly. The people shall have the right peaceably to assemble, petition for redress or peaceably protest governmental action

Convention Notes

No change except in grammar [Art III, see 26] Retains basic rights to assemble and to petition or protest for redress of grievances

Section 7   Freedom of speech, expression, and press. No law shall be passed impairing the freedom of speech or expression Every person shall be free to speak or publish whatever he will on any subject, being responsible for all abuse of that liberty In all suits and prosecutions for libel or slander the truth thereof may be given in evidence, and the jury, under the direction of the court, shall determine the law and the facts

Compiler's Notes

Section 3 of the Transition Schedule provides that "rights, procedural or substantive, created for the first time by Article II shall be prospective and not retroactive"

Convention Notes

Revises 1889 constitution [Art III, see 10] by enlarging a citizen's freedom to express himself and allowing the truth to be given in evidence in slander as well as libel cases

Cross-References

Criminal libel, see 94 2801 et seq
Defamation, libel and slander defined, see 61 202 et seq
Political criminal libel, see 94-1454

Section 8.   Right of participation The public has the right to expect governmental agencies to afford such reasonable opportunity for citizen participation in the operation of the agencies prior to the final decision as may be provided by law.

Compiler's Notes

Section 3 of the Transition Schedule provides that "rights, procedural or substantive, created for the first time by Article II shall be prospective and not retroactive

Convention Notes

New provision creating a right of the people to participate in the decision making process of state and local government

Section 9   Right to know No person shall be deprived of the right to examine documents or to observe the deliberations of all public bodies or agencies of state government and its subdivisions, except in cases in which the demand of individual privacy clearly exceeds the merits of public disclosure

Compiler's Notes

Section 3 of the Transition Schedule provides that "rights, procedural or substantive, created for the first time by Article II shall be prospective and not retroactive"

Convention Notes

New provision that government documents and operations be open to public scrutiny except when the right to know is outweighed by the right to individual privacy

Section 10.   Right of privacy The right of individual privacy is essential to the well-being of a free society and shall not be infringed without the showing of a compelling state interest

Compiler's Notes

Section 3 of the Transition Schedule provides that "rights, procedural or substantive, created for the first time by Article II shall be prospective and not retroactive.'

Convention Notes

New provision prohibiting any invasion of privacy unless the good of the state makes it necessary

3

Section 11   Searches and seizures. The people shall be secure in their persons, papers, homes and effects from unreasonable searches and seizures No warrant to search any place, or seize any person or thing shall issue without describing the place to be searched or the person or thing to be seized, or without probable cause supported by oath or affirmation reduced to writing

Convention Notes

Identical to 1889 constitution [Art III, see 7]

Cross-References

Motion to suppress evidence illegally seized, see 95-1806
Search and seizure, procedural requirements, see 95-701 et seq

Section 12   Right to bear arms. The right of any person to keep or bear arms in defense of his own home person, and property, or in aid of the civil power when thereto legally summoned, shall not be called in question, but nothing herein contained shall be held to permit the carrying of concealed weapons

Convention Notes

Identical to 1889 constitution [Art III, sec. 13]

Section 13   Right of suffrage. All elections shall be free and open, and no power, civil or military, shall at any time interfere to prevent the free exercise of the right of suffrage

Convention Notes

Identical to 1889 constitution [Art III, sec 5]

Section 14.   Adult rights. A person 18 years of age or older is an adult for all purposes

Compiler's Notes

Section 3 of the Transition Schedule provides that "rights, procedural or substantive, created for the first time by Article II shall be prospective and not retroactive '

Convention Notes

New provision Self explanatory

Cross-References

Minors and adults defined, see 64 101

Section 15.   Rights of persons not adults. The rights of persons under 18 years of age shall include, but not be limited to, all the fundamental rights of this Article unless specifically precluded by laws which enhance the protection of such persons

Compiler's Notes

Section 3 of the Transition Schedule provides that ' rights, procedural or substantive, created for the first time by Article II shall be prospective and not retroactive "

Convention Notes

New provision giving children all of the rights that adults have unless a law meant to protect children prohibits their enjoyment of the right

Section 16.   The administration of justice Courts of justice shall be open to every person, and speedy remedy afforded for every injury of person, property, or character No person shall be deprived of this full legal redress for injury incurred in employment for which another person

may be liable except as to fellow employees and his immediate employer
who hired him if such immediate employer provides coverage under the
Workmen's Compensation Laws of this state. Right and justice shall be
administered without sale, denial, or delay.

Compiler's Notes

Section 3 of the Transition Schedule
provides that "rights, procedural or substantive, created for the first time by
Article II shall be prospective and not
retroactive."

Convention Notes

Adds to 1889 constitution [Art III, sec
6] by specifically granting to a person
injured in employment the right to sue a

third party causing the injury, except his
employer or fellow employee when his
employer provides coverage under workmen's compensation laws

Cross-References

Workmen's compensation, election of employer and employee to come under act,
action against third party causing injury,
see 92-204

Section 17   Due process of law   No person shall be deprived of life,
liberty, or property without due process of law

Convention Notes

Identical to 1889 constitution [Art III,
sec 27]

Section 18   State subject to suit.   The state, counties, cities, towns
and all other local governmental entities shall have no immunity from suit
for injury to a person or property. This provision shall apply only to
causes of action arising after July 1, 1973

Compiler's Notes

Section 3 of the Transition Schedule
provides that "rights, procedural or substantive, created for the first time by
Article II shall be prospective and not
retroactive."

Convention Notes

New provision abolishing the doctrine of
sovereign immunity ("the King can do

no wrong") and allowing any person to
sue the state and local governments for
injuries caused by officials and employees
thereof

Cross-References

Sovereign immunity defense prohibited
when liability of political subdivision in-
sured, see 40-4102

Section 19   Habeas corpus   The privilege of the writ of habeas corpus
shall never be suspended

Compiler's Notes

Section 3 of the Transition Schedule
provides that "rights, procedural or substantive, created for the first time by
Article II shall be prospective and not
retroactive."

Convention Notes

Revises 1889 constitution [Art III sec
21] which allowed the writ of habeas
corpus to be suspended in case of rebellion

or invasion. Revision provides that the
writ (the right to test the lawfulness of a
person's being detained) may never be
suspended

Cross References

Habeas corpus, scope and procedure, see
95-2701 et seq
Supreme court jurisdiction, Const Art
VII, sec 2

Section 20   Initiation of proceedings   (1) Criminal offenses within
the jurisdiction of any court inferior to the district court shall be prosecuted by complaint. All criminal actions in district court, except those on
appeal shall be prosecuted either by information after examination and

5

commitment by a magistrate or after leave granted by the court, or by indictment without such examination, commitment or leave

(2) A grand jury shall consist of eleven persons, of whom eight must concur to find an indictment A grand jury shall be drawn and summoned only at the discretion and order of the district judge

Convention Notes

Returns method in 1889 constitution [Art III, sec 8] of starting criminal actions Increases grand jury from seven to eleven persons

Grand jury, summoning, powers and duties, sec 95 1401 et seq

Methods of prosecution, procedure, see 95-1501 et seq

Cross-References

Grand jury, composition and drawing, sec 93-1801 et seq

Section 21   Bail All persons shall be bailable by sufficient sureties, except for capital offenses, when the proof is evident or the presumption great

Compiler's Notes

A separately submitted proposition against the death penalty which would have deleted from this section "except for capital offenses, when the proof is evident or the presumption great" was not adopted by the electorate

Convention Notes

Identical to 1889 constitution [Art III, sec 19] Guarantees that all persons are bailable except in case of certain offenses punishable by death

Cross-References

Bail, purpose, procedure, sec 95-1101 et seq

Section 22   Excessive sanctions Excessive bail shall not be required, or excessive fines imposed, or cruel and unusual punishments inflicted

Convention Notes

Identical to 1889 constitution [Art III, sec 20]

Section 23   Detention No person shall be imprisoned for the purpose of securing his testimony in any criminal proceeding longer than may be necessary in order to take his deposition If he can give security for his appearance at the time of trial, he shall be discharged upon giving the same, if he cannot give security, his deposition shall be taken in the manner provided by law, and in the presence of the accused and his counsel, or without their presence, if they shall fail to attend the examination after reasonable notice of the time and place thereof.

Convention Notes

Deleted provision in 1889 constitution [Art III, sec 17] that depositions may be used in a trial if the witness who gave it is dead or out of state Retained language is identical to 1889 constitution

Cross-References

Depositions in criminal cases, sec 95 1802

Section 24   Rights of the accused In all criminal prosecutions the accused shall have the right to appear and defend in person and by counsel, to demand the nature and cause of the accusation, to meet the witnesses against him face to face to have process to compel the attendance of

6

witnesses in his behalf, and a speedy public trial by an impartial jury of the county or district in which the offense is alleged to have been committed, subject to the right of the state to have a change of venue for any of the causes for which the defendant may obtain the same.

Convention Notes

Identical to 1889 constitution [Art III, sec 16] Establishes fundamental procedural rights of a person accused of crime

Cross References

Change of place of trial when fair trial cannot be had in county, sec 95-1710

Confessions obtained by duress or inhuman practices, misdemeanor, secs 94-3918, 94-3919

Examination of witnesses on commission, see 94-9201 et seq

Form of charge, sec 95-1503

Method of trial, sec 95 1901 et seq

Rights of defendant in a criminal action, see 94-4806

Right to counsel, sec 95-1001 et seq

Subpoenas, see 95-1801

Uniform Act to Secure the Attendance of Witnesses from Without the State in Criminal Cases, sec 94 9001 et seq

Section 25   Self-incrimination and double jeopardy. No person shall be compelled to testify against himself in a criminal proceeding No person shall be again put in jeopardy for the same offense previously tried in any jurisdiction

Compiler's Notes

Section 3 of the Transition Schedule provides that "rights, procedural or substantive, created for the first time by Article II shall be prospective and not retroactive"

Convention Notes

Revises 1889 constitution [Art III, see 18] by protecting a person from being tried for the same crime by both this state and the United States or another state.

Cross-References

Defense of former prosecution, when allowed, exceptions, see 94-6808 1 et seq

Protection of witnesses against self-incrimination, see 93-2101 2

Section 26   Trial by jury. The right of trial by jury is secured to all and shall remain inviolate But upon default of appearance or by consent of the parties expressed in such manner as the law may provide, all cases may be tried without a jury or before fewer than the number of jurors provided by law In all civil actions, two-thirds of the jury may render a verdict, and a verdict so rendered shall have the same force and effect as if all had concurred therein In all criminal actions, the verdict shall be unanimous

Compiler's Notes

Section 3 of the Transition Schedule provides that "rights, procedural or substantive, created for the first time by Article II shall be prospective and not retroactive"

Convention Notes

Revises 1889 constitution [Art III, sec 23] by permitting a defendant to waive a jury trial in felony cases as well as civil and misdemeanor cases and by requiring all jurors (rather than 2/3) agree before a defendant may be convicted of a misdemeanor

Cross-References

Civil cases, jury trial of right, M R Civ P, Rule 38

Criminal cases, method of trial in district court, sec 95-1901 et seq

Criminal cases, method of trial in justice and police courts, see 95 2004 et seq

Section 27   Imprisonment for debt No person shall be imprisoned for debt except in the manner provided by law, upon refusal to deliver up

7

his estate for the benefit of his creditors, or in cases of tort where there is strong presumption of fraud

Convention Notes

Identical to 1889 constitution [Art III, sec 12] Safeguards the right of a person in debt to be free from imprisonment

Section 28   Rights of the convicted Laws for the punishment of crime shall be founded on the principles of prevention and reformation Full rights are restored by termination of state supervision for any offense against the state

Compiler's Notes

Section 3 of the Transition Schedule provides that 'rights, procedural or substantive, created for the first time by Article II shall be prospective and not retroactive.'

A separately submitted proposition which would have added the following sentence to this section ' Death shall not be prescribed as a penalty for any crime against the state' was not adopted by the electorate

Convention Notes

Revises 1889 constitution [Art III, sec 24] by deleting reference to capital punishment and providing that rights a person loses when convicted of a crime are automatically restored when he has served his sentence

Cross References

Civil rights of convict suspended, civil death, limitations, sec 94 4720 et seq

Execution of sentence see 95 2301 et seq

Inhumanity to prisoners, penalty, see 94-3017

Sentence and judgment, sec 95 2201 et seq

Section 29   Eminent domain Private property shall not be taken or damaged for public use without just compensation to the full extent of the loss having been first made to or paid into court for the owner In the event of litigation, just compensation shall include necessary expenses of litigation to be awarded by the court when the private property owner prevails

Compiler's Notes

Section 3 of the Transition Schedule provides that "rights, procedural or substantive created for the first time by Article II shall be prospective and not retroactive"

Convention Notes

Retains provisions in 1889 constitution [Art III, sec 14] on eminent domain and expands its protection by guaranteeing that a property owner who goes to court and is awarded more money than offered for his property being condemned will be reimbursed for the necessary expenses of the lawsuit (such as appraiser and attorneys fees)

Cross References

Eminent domain, procedure, see 93 9901 et seq

Section 30.   Treason and descent of estates Treason against the state shall consist only in levying war against it, or in adhering to its enemies, giving them aid and comfort, no person shall be convicted of treason except on the testimony of two witnesses to the same overt act, or on his confession in open court no person shall be attainted of treason or felony by the legislature, no conviction shall cause the loss of property to the relatives or heirs of the convicted The estates of suicides shall descend or vest as in cases of natural death

Convention Notes
No change except in grammar [Art III, sec 9]

Cross-References
Evidence on trial for treason, secs 93-1401-2, 94-7210
Treason and misprision of treason, secs 94-4301, 94 4502

Section 31 Ex post facto, obligation of contracts, and irrevocable privileges No ex post facto law nor any law impairing the obligation of contracts or making any irrevocable grant of special privileges, franchises, or immunities, shall be passed by the legislature

Convention Notes
Identical to 1889 constitution [Art III, sec 11]

Section 32 Civilian control of the military The military shall always be in strict subordination to the civil power, no soldier shall in time of peace be quartered in any house without the consent of the owner, nor in time of war except in the manner provided by law

Convention Notes
Identical to 1889 constitution [Art III, sec 22]

Section 33 Importation of armed persons. No armed person or persons or armed body of men shall be brought into this state for the preservation of the peace, or the suppression of domestic violence, except upon the application of the legislature, or of the governor when the legislature cannot be convened

Convention Notes
Identical to 1889 constitution [Art III, sec 31]

Section 34 Unenumerated rights The enumeration in this constitution of certain rights shall not be construed to deny, impair, or disparage others retained by the people

Convention Notes
Identical to 1889 constitution [Art III, sec 30]

Section 35 Servicemen, servicewomen, and veterans. The people declare that Montana servicemen, servicewomen, and veterans may be given special considerations determined by the legislature.

Compiler's Notes
Section 3 of the Transition Schedule provides that "rights, procedural or substantive, created for the first time by Article II shall be prospective and not retroactive "

Convention Notes
New provision allowing legislature to give servicemen, servicewomen, and veterans special treatment in the law

ARTICLE III

GENERAL GOVERNMENT

Section 1   Separation of powers. The power of the government of this state is divided into three distinct branches—legislative, executive, and judicial No person or persons charged with the exercise of power properly belonging to one branch shall exercise any power properly belonging to either of the others, except as in this constitution expressly directed or permitted

Convention Notes

Identical to 1889 constitution [Art IV, see 1] except for substitution of the word "branches" for "departments" This distinguishes the three branches of government from the 20 departments in the executive branch

Section 2   Continuity of government The seat of government shall be in Helena, except during periods of emergency resulting from disasters or enemy attack The legislature may enact laws to insure the continuity of government during a period of emergency without regard for other provisions of the constitution They shall be effective only during the period of emergency that affects a particular office or governmental operation.

Convention Notes

Revises 1889 constitution [Art X sec 3] by removing provision which allowed seat of government to be moved by a vote of 2/3 of the people No other change except in grammar [See also 1889 constitution Art V, see 46]

Cross-References

Continuity in government, post enemy attack, see 82-3801 et seq.

Section 3   Oath of office. Members of the legislature and all executive, ministerial and judicial officers, shall take and subscribe the following oath or affirmation, before they enter upon the duties of their offices "I do solemnly swear (or affirm) that I will support, protect and defend the constitution of the United States, and the constitution of the state of Montana, and that I will discharge the duties of my office with fidelity (so help me God) " No other oath, declaration, or test shall be required as a qualification for any office or public trust

Convention Notes

Shortened version of oath contained in 1889 constitution [Art XIX, sec 1]

Cross-References

Acting in public capacity without having qualified misdemeanor, sec. 94-3901
Form of oath, filing, sec 59 413 et seq

Section 4   Initiative (1) The people may enact laws by initiative on all matters except appropriations of money and local or special laws

(2) Initiative petitions must contain the full text of the proposed measure, shall be signed by at least five percent of the qualified electors in each of at least one-third of the legislative representative districts and the total number of signers must be at least five percent of the total qualified electors of the state Petitions shall be filed with the secretary of state at least three months prior to the election at which the measure will be voted upon

(3) The sufficiency of the initiative petition shall not be questioned after the election is held

Convention Notes

Revises 1889 constitution [Art V, sec 1] by requiring a petition to be signed by 5% of electors in 1/3 of the legislative districts instead of 8% in 2/5 of the counties

Cross-References

Form of petition, procedure, see 37-102 et seq

Reservation of powers of initiative and referendum, Const Art V, sec. 1

Section 5. Referendum. (1) The people may approve or reject by referendum any act of the legislature except an appropriation of money A referendum shall be held either upon order by the legislature or upon petition signed by at least five percent of the qualified electors in each of at least one-third of the legislative representative districts The total number of signers must be at least five percent of the qualified electors of the state A referendum petition shall be filed with the secretary of state no later than six months after adjournment of the legislature which passed the act.

(2) An act referred to the people is in effect until suspended by petitions signed by at least 15 percent of the qualified electors in a majority of the legislative representative districts. If so suspended the act shall become operative only after it is approved at an election, the result of which has been determined and declared as provided by law

Convention Notes

Revises 1889 constitution [Art V, sec 1] by allowing people to vote on any act of the legislature except appropriations and by requiring referendum petitions to be signed by 5% of the electors in 1/3 of the legislative districts instead of 8% of the electors in 2/5 of the counties (1889 Constitution does not allow referen dums on laws "necessary for the immediate preservation of the public peace, health, or safety")

Cross-References

Form of petition, procedure, secs 37-101, 37-103 et seq

Reservation of powers of initiative and referendum, Const Art V, sec. 1

Section 6   Elections. The people shall vote on initiative and referendum measures at the general election unless the legislature orders a special election.

Convention Notes

No change except in grammar [Art V, sec 1]

Section 7. Number of electors. The number of qualified electors required in each legislative representative district and in the state shall be determined by the number of votes cast for the office of governor in the preceding general election

Convention Notes

No change except in grammar [Art V, sec. 1]

Section 8   Prohibition. The provisions of this Article do not apply to CONSTITUTIONAL REVISION, Article XIV

Convention Notes

New provision which differentiates the general initiative and referendum re-quirements from the special initiative and referendum requirements for amending the constitution

Section 9   Gambling All forms of gambling, lotteries, and gift enterprises are prohibited unless authorized by acts of the legislature or by the people through initiative or referendum

Compiler's Notes

This section became a part of the constitution is the result of the approval by the electorate of a separately submitted provision The adoption added "unless authorized by acts of the legislature or by the people through initiative or referendum"

Convention Notes

Adds the word "gambling" to language of 1889 constitution [Art XIX, sec 2] Makes it clear that all forms of gambling are prohibited [See Compiler's Notes, above]

ARTICLE IV

SUFFRAGE AND ELECTIONS

Section 1   Ballot. All elections by the people shall be by secret ballot

Convention Notes

Revises 1889 constitution [Art IX, sec 1] by adding the word "secret"

Cross-References

Elections to be by ballot, see 23 2602

Section 2   Qualified elector. Any citizen of the United States 18 years of age or older who meets the registration and residence requirements provided by law is a qualified elector unless he is serving a sentence for a felony in a penal institution or is of unsound mind, as determined by a court

Convention Notes

Revises 1889 constitution [Art IX, secs 2, 3, 6, 8, 12] Provides legislative rather than constitutional requirements for residence and registration Convicted felon loses voting rights only while incarcerated (18 is voting age established

for ALL elections by 26th amendment to U S constitution ratified June 30, 1971)

Cross References

Attempting to vote without being qualified, misdemeanor, see 94 1404

Qualifications of voters, see 23 2701

Section 3   Elections The legislature shall provide by law the requirements for residence, registration, absentee voting, and administration of elections It may provide for a system of poll booth registration, and shall insure the purity of elections and guard against abuses of the electoral process

Convention Notes

Revises 1889 constitution [Art IX, secs 2, 9] Provides legislative rather than constitutional establishment of requirements which are often affected by (and sometimes in conflict with) federal law and court decisions When necessary to comply with federal requirements it is much easier to change the law than to amend the constitution Second sentence specifically authorizes legislature to provide for voter registration at time and

place of voting—rather than in advance of election

Cross References

Absentee voting and registration, secs 23 3006, 23-3701 et seq

Election frauds and offenses see 94 1101 et seq

Elections, definitions and general provisions, sec 23 2601 et seq

Registration of electors, see 23 3001 et seq

Section 4   Eligibility for public office. Any qualified elector is eligible to any public office except as otherwise provided in this constitution

12

The legislature may provide additional qualifications but no person convicted of a felony shall be eligible to hold office until his final discharge from state supervision

Convention Notes

Revises 1889 constitution [Art IX, secs 10, 11] by providing that a felon's right to seek public office is automatically restored after serving sentence

Cross-References

Disqualifications and restrictions, see 59-301 et seq

Section 5. Result of elections. In all elections held by the people, the person or persons receiving the largest number of votes shall be declared elected

Convention Notes

No change except in grammar [Art IX, sec 13]

Cross References

Determination of candidate elected, see 23-2003

Section 6 Privilege from arrest A qualified elector is privileged from arrest at polling places and in going to and returning therefrom, unless apprehended in the commission of a felony or a breach of the peace.

Convention Notes

1889 constitution [Art IX, sec 4] reworded Voter is immune from arrest during the voting process unless during such time he commits a felony or breach of peace

Cross References

Privilege from arrest, secs 23-2705, 95-616

ARTICLE V

THE LEGISLATURE

Section 1. Power and structure. The legislative power is vested in a legislature consisting of a senate and a house of representatives The people reserve to themselves the powers of initiative and referendum

Compiler's Notes

Section 2 of the Transition Schedule provides that this section shall not become effective until the date the first redistricting and reapportionment plan becomes law

A separately submitted proposition concerning a unicameral legislature, was not adopted by the electorate

Convention Notes

No change except in grammar [Art V, sec 1]

Cross References

Composition of legislative assembly see 43-201

Initiative, Const Art III, sec 4.
Referendum, Const Art III, sec 5

Section 2. Size The size of the legislature shall be provided by law but the senate shall not have more than 50 or fewer than 40 members and the house shall not have more than 100 or fewer than 80 members

Compiler's Notes

Section 2 of the Transition Schedule provides that this section shall not become effective until the date the first redistricting and reapportionment plan becomes law

Convention Notes

New provision for determining size of legislature

13

Section 3   Election and terms   A member of the house of representatives shall be elected for a term of two years and a member of the
senate for a term of four years each to begin on a date provided by law
One-half of the senators shall be elected every two years

Compiler's Notes

Section 2 of the Transition Schedule
provides that this section shall not become
effective until the date the first redistricting and reapportionment plan becomes
law

Section 5 of the Transition Schedule
provides

"(1) The terms of all legislators elected
before the effective date of this Constitution shall end on December 31 of the year

in which the first redistricting and reapportionment plan becomes law

"(2) The senators first elected under
this Constitution shall draw lots to establish a term of two years for one-half of
their number"

Convention Notes

Revises 1889 constitution [Art V, sec
2] by adding requirement for staggered
terms for senators

Section 4   Qualifications   A candidate for the legislature shall be a
resident of the state for at least one year next preceding the general election For six months next preceding the general election, he shall be a
resident of the county if it contains one or more districts or of the district if it contains all or parts of more than one county

Convention Notes

Revises 1889 constitution [Art V, sec
3] by reducing district or county resi-

dency requirements from one year to six
months and eliminating age requirements

Section 5.   Compensation   Each member of the legislature shall receive compensation for his services and allowances provided by law No
legislature may fix its own compensation

Convention Notes

No change except in grammar [Art V,
sec 5]

Cross-References

Per diem, mileage and expenses of members, sec. 43-310

Section 6.   Sessions   The legislature shall be a continuous body for
two-year periods beginning when newly elected members take office Any
business, bill, or resolution pending at adjournment of a session shall
carry over with the same status to any other session of the legislature
during the biennium The legislature shall meet at least once a year in
regular session of not more than 60 legislative days Any legislature may
increase the limit on the length of any subsequent session The legislature
may be convened in special sessions by the governor or at the written
request of a majority of the members

Compiler's Notes

Section 1 of the Transition Schedule
provides that this section shall be effective
January 1, 1973

Convention Notes

New provision "Continuous body" does
not mean the legislature is in continuous
session but means the legislature has

legal existence even when not actually
meeting It will have regular annual sessions of 60 days. A legislature cannot pass
a law that IT can meet for more than 60
legislative days but can provide that
future legislatures may meet longer Legislature as well as the governor may call
a special session [See 1889 constitution
Art V, secs 5, 6]

Section 7   Vacancies.   A vacancy in the legislature shall be filled by
special election for the unexpired term unless otherwise provided by law

Convention Notes

New provision which would require filling vacancies by election if the present law requiring appointments is ever repealed

Cross-References

Vacancies, how filled, see 59 601 et seq

Section 8. Immunity A member of the legislature is privileged from arrest during attendance at sessions of the legislature and in going to and returning therefrom, unless apprehended in the commission of a felony or a breach of the peace He shall not be questioned in any other place for any speech or debate in the legislature

Convention Notes

No change except in grammar [Art. V, sec 15]

Cross-References

Privilege from arrest, see 95 616

Section 9. Disqualification. No member of the legislature shall, during the term for which he shall have been elected, be appointed to any civil office under the state, and no member of congress, or other person holding an office (except notary public, or the militia) under the United States or this state, shall be a member of the legislature during his continuance in office

Convention Notes

No change except in grammar [Art V, sec 7].

Section 10 Organization and procedure (1) Each house shall judge the election and qualifications of its members It may by law vest in the courts the power to try and determine contested elections Each house shall choose its officers from among its members, keep a journal, and make rules for its proceedings Each house may expel or punish a member for good cause shown with the concurrence of two-thirds of all its members

(2) A majority of each house constitutes a quorum A smaller number may adjourn from day to day and compel attendance of absent members

(3) The sessions of the legislature and of the committee of the whole, all committee meetings, and all hearings shall be open to the public.

(4) The legislature may establish a legislative council and other interim committees The legislature shall establish a legislative post-audit committee which shall supervise post-auditing duties provided by law.

(5) Neither house shall, without the consent of the other, adjourn or recess for more than three days or to any place other than that in which the two houses are sitting.

Convention Notes

(1) and (2) no change except in grammar [Art V, secs 10, 11, 12] (3) Revises 1889 constitution [Art V, sec. 13] by preventing the legislature from conducting secret proceedings (4) New provision specifically allowing the legislature to create committees to work between the annual meetings (5) No change except in grammar [Art V, sec 14]

Cross-References

Disturbing legislative assembly while in session, misdemeanor, sec 94-2902

Legislative council, sec 43-709 et seq

Preventing meeting or organization of legislative assembly, felony, sec 94-2901

Section 11. Bills. (1) A law shall be passed by bill which shall not be so altered or amended on its passage through the legislature as to change its original purpose No bill shall become law except by a vote of the majority of all members present and voting

(2) Every vote of each member of the legislature on each substantive question in the legislature, in any committee, or in committee of the whole shall be recorded and made public On final passage, the vote shall be taken by ayes and noes and the names entered on the journal

(3) Each bill, except general appropriation bills and bills for the codification and general revision of the laws, shall contain only one subject, clearly expressed in its title If any subject is embraced in any act and is not expressed in the title, only so much of the act not so expressed is void

(4) A general appropriation bill shall contain only appropriations for the ordinary expenses of the legislative, executive, and judicial branches for interest on the public debt, and for public schools Every other appropriation shall be made by a separate bill, containing but one subject

(5) No appropriation shall be made for religious, charitable, industrial educational, or benevolent purposes to any private individual, private association, or private corporation not under control of the state

(6) A law may be challenged on the ground of noncompliance with this section only within two years after its effective date

Convention Notes

(1) No change except in grammar [Art V, sec 19] (2) Changes 1889 constitution [Art V, sec 21] by requiring recorded votes on all actions which affect passage of a bill (3) (4) (5) No change except in grammar [Art V, secs 23, 33, 35] (6) New provision After it is two years old a law cannot be challenged in court because of technical errors in the way it was passed

Cross-References

Altering draft or engrossed or enrolled copy of bill or resolution, felony, secs 94 2903 94 2904

Bribery of members of legislative assembly, penalties, see 94 2905 et seq

Journals, how authenticated, sec 43-304

Personal interest of member in bill, misdemeanor, sec 94 2911

Section 12. Local and special legislation The legislature shall not pass a special or local act when a general act is or can be made, applicable

Convention Notes

No change except in grammar [Art V, sec 26]

Section 13 Impeachment (1) The governor, executive officers, heads of state departments judicial officers, and such other officers as may be provided by law are subject to impeachment, and upon conviction shall be removed from office Other proceedings for removal from public office for cause may be provided by law

(2) The legislature shall provide for the manner, procedure, and causes for impeachment and may select the senate as tribunal

(3) Impeachment shall be brought only by a two-thirds vote of the house The tribunal hearing the charges shall convict only by a vote of two-thirds or more of its members

(4) Conviction shall extend only to removal from office, but the party, whether convicted or acquitted, shall also be liable to prosecution according to law

Convention Notes

Minor revision [Art V, secs 16, 17, 18] Two thirds rather than a majority vote necessary to impeach The legislature may choose the senate or another body to hear the charges

Cross References

Conviction of crime, forfeiture of office, see 94-2914

Impeachment, procedure, see 94-5401 et seq

Removal of officers otherwise than by impeachment, see 94-5501 et seq

Section 14   Districting and apportionment   (1) The state shall be divided into as many districts as there are members of the house, and each district shall elect one representative Each senate district shall be composed of two adjoining house districts, and shall elect one senator. Each district shall consist of compact and contiguous territory All districts shall be as nearly equal in population as is practicable

(2) In the legislative session following ratification of this constitution and thereafter in each session preceding each federal population census, a commission of five citizens, none of whom may be public officials, shall be selected to prepare a plan for redistricting and reapportioning the state into legislative and congressional districts The majority and minority leaders of each house shall each designate one commissioner Within 20 days after their designation, the four commissioners shall select the fifth member, who shall serve as chairman of the commission If the four members fail to select the fifth member within the time prescribed, a majority of the supreme court shall select him

(3) The commission shall submit its plan to the legislature at the first regular session after its appointment or after the census figures are available. Within 30 days after submission, the legislature shall return the plan to the commission with its recommendations Within 30 days thereafter, the commission shall file its final plan with the secretary of state and it shall become law The commission is then dissolved

Compiler's Notes

Section 1 of the Transition Schedule provides that this section shall be effective January 1, 1973

Convention Notes

(1) New provision for single member house districts Two house districts constitute a senatorial district (2) and (3)

new provision which establishes a five member commission to recommend a reapportionment plan after each U S census [See 1889 constitution Art VI, secs 2, 3]

Cross-References

Senatorial, representative and congressional districts, see 43-106 6 et seq

ARTICLE VI

THE EXECUTIVE

Section 1   Officers.   (1) The executive branch includes a governor, lieutenant governor, secretary of state, attorney general, superintendent of public instruction, and auditor

(2) Each holds office for a term of four years which begins on the first Monday of January next succeeding election, and until a successor is elected and qualified.

(3) Each shall reside at the seat of government, there keep the public records of his office, and perform such other duties as are provided in this constitution and by law

Convention Notes

Revises 1889 constitution [Art VII, secs 1-8, 20] Removes constitutional status of state treasurer, board of examiners, and state examiner The offices still appear in the law All officers mentioned must reside at capital 1889 constitution exempts lieutenant governor from this requirement

Section 2. Election. (1) The governor, lieutenant governor, secretary of state, attorney general, superintendent of public instruction, and auditor shall be elected by the qualified electors at a general election provided by law

(2) Each candidate for governor shall file jointly with a candidate for lieutenant governor in primary elections, or so otherwise comply with nomination procedures provided by law that the offices of governor and lieutenant governor are voted upon together in primary and general elections.

Convention Notes

Only change [Art VII, sec 2] is subsection (2) which is new requirement that governor and lieutenant governor must run as a team

Section 3 Qualifications. (1) No person shall be eligible to the office of governor, lieutenant governor, secretary of state, attorney general, superintendent of public instruction, or auditor unless he is 25 years of age or older at the time of his election In addition, each shall be a citizen of the United States who has resided within the state two years next preceding his election

(2) Any person with the foregoing qualifications is eligible to the office of attorney general if an attorney in good standing admitted to practice law in Montana who has engaged in the active practice thereof for at least five years before election

(3) The superintendent of public instruction shall have such educational qualifications as are provided by law

Convention Notes

Revises 1889 constitution [Art VII, sec 3] Sets 25 as age requirement for governor, lieutenant governor, superintendent of public instruction and attorney general Age requirement for secretary of state unchanged New requirements that candidate for attorney general be admitted to practice law for five years and superintendent of public instruction have educational qualifications set by law

Cross-References

Superintendent of public instruction, qualifications, sec 75-5702

Section 4 Duties (1) The executive power is vested in the governor who shall see that the laws are faithfully executed He shall have such other duties as are provided in this constitution and by law

(2) The lieutenant governor shall perform the duties provided by law and those delegated to him by the governor No power specifically vested

18

in the governor by this constitution may be delegated to the lieutenant governor

(3) The secretary of state shall maintain official records of the executive branch and of the acts of the legislature, as provided by law He shall keep the great seal of the state of Montana and perform any other duties provided by law

(4) The attorney general is the legal officer of the state and shall have the duties and powers provided by law

(5) The superintendent of public instruction and the auditor shall have such duties as are provided by law.

Convention Notes

Only change [Art VII, secs 1, 5, 15, 17] is subsection (2) which is new provision allowing legislature to make lieutenant governor full time Deletes provision that lieutenant governor be president of senate

Cross-References

Attorney general, duties see 82-401
Governor, powers and duties, sec 82-1301

Lieutenant governor, duties, compensation, see 82 1701 et seq

Secretary of state, custody of records, duties, see 82 2201 et seq

State auditor, general fiscal duties, see 79 101

Superintendent of public instruction, election, duties, see 75 5701 et seq

Section 5. Compensation. (1) Officers of the executive branch shall receive salaries provided by law

(2) During his term, no elected officer of the executive branch may hold another public office or receive compensation for services from any other governmental agency He may be a candidate for any public office during his term

Convention Notes

Revises 1889 constitution [Art VII, see 4] Salaries may be increased or decreased Public official may not receive more than one salary or hold more than

one office but may be candidate for an other office without resigning

Cross-References

Salaries of elected state officials, see 25-501

Section 6   Vacancy in office. (1)   If the office of lieutenant governor becomes vacant by his succession to the office of governor, or by his death, resignation, or disability as determined by law, the governor shall appoint a qualified person to serve in that office for the remainder of the term If both the elected governor and the elected lieutenant governor become unable to serve in the office of governor, succession to the respective offices shall be as provided by law for the period until the next general election Then, a governor and lieutenant governor shall be elected to fill the remainder of the original term

(2) If the office of secretary of state attorney general, auditor, or superintendent of public instruction becomes vacant by death resignation, or disability as determined by law the governor shall appoint a qualified person to serve in that office until the next general election and until a successor is elected and qualified The person elected to fill a vacancy shall hold the office until the expiration of the term for which his predecessor was elected

Convention Notes

Revises 1889 constitution [Art VII, secs 7, 15, 16] by changing method of filling vacancy in office of lieutenant governor Senate confirmation no longer required for appointments to fill vacancies in offices listed

Cross-References

Resignation and vacancies, see 59 601 et seq

Section 7   20 departments   All executive and administrative offices, boards, bureaus, commissions agencies and instrumentalities of the executive branch (except for the office of governor, lieutenant governor, secretary of state attorney general, superintendent of public instruction, and auditor) and their respective functions, powers, and duties, shall be allocated by law among not more than 20 principal departments so as to provide an orderly arrangement in the administrative organization of state government Temporary commissions may be established by law and need not be allocated within a department

Convention Notes

Only grammar change in 20 department reorganization amendment [Art VII, sec 21] adopted by the people in November, 1970

Cross-References

Reorganization of executive department, Title 82A

Section 8   Appointing power   (1) The departments provided for in section 7 shall be under the supervision of the governor Except as otherwise provided in this constitution or by law, each department shall be headed by a single executive appointed by the governor subject to confirmation by the senate to hold office until the end of the governor's term unless sooner removed by the governor

(2) The governor shall appoint, subject to confirmation by the senate, all officers provided for in this constitution or by law whose appointment or election is not otherwise provided for They shall hold office until the end of the governor's term unless sooner removed by the governor

(3) If a vacancy occurs in any such office when the legislature is not in session, the governor shall appoint a qualified person to discharge the duties thereof until the office is filled by appointment and confirmation

(4) A person not confirmed by the senate for an office shall not except at its request, be nominated again for that office at the same session, or be appointed to that office when the legislature is not in session

Convention Notes

Subsection (1) new provision Unless law provides otherwise governor appoints heads of the 20 departments, subject to senate confirmation No change except in grammar in subsections (2) and (3) [Art VII, sec 7] Subsection (4) is new provision prohibiting nomination or appointment of persons previously rejected by senate

Section 9   Budget and messages   The governor shall at the beginning of each legislative session, and may at other times, give the legislature information and recommend measures he considers necessary The governor shall submit to the legislature at a time fixed by law, a budget for the ensuing fiscal period setting forth in detail for all operating funds the proposed expenditures and estimated revenue of the state

Convention Notes

Makes it mandatory that Governor send budget to legislature Otherwise no change except in grammar [Art VII, sec 10]

Cross-References

Budget, submission to legislature, form, contents, see 79 1015

Section 10   Veto power   (1) Each bill passed by the legislature, except bills proposing amendments to the Montana constitution, bills ratifying proposed amendments to the United States constitution, resolutions, and initiative and referendum measures shall be submitted to the governor for his signature If he does not sign or veto the bill within five days after its delivery to him if the legislature is in session or within 25 days if the legislature is adjourned, it shall become law The governor shall return a vetoed bill to the legislature with a statement of his reasons therefor

(2) The governor may return any bill to the legislature with his recommendation for amendment If the legislature passes the bill in accordance with the governor's recommendation, it shall again return the bill to the governor for his reconsideration The governor shall not return a bill for amendment a second time

(3) If after receipt of a veto message, two-thirds of the members present approve the bill, it shall become law

(4) If the legislature is not in session when the governor vetoes a bill, he shall return the bill with his reasons therefor to the legislature as provided by law The legislature may reconvene to reconsider any bill so vetoed

(5) The governor may veto items in appropriation bills and in such instances the procedure shall be the same as upon veto of an entire bill

Convention Notes

Subsection (1) revises 1889 constitution [Art VII, sec 12] Amendments to U S and Montana constitutions and legislative resolutions may be passed without governor's signature Pocket veto after adjournment eliminated Subsection (2) new provision "Amendatory veto' enables governor to return bills with suggestions for changes No change in subsection (3)

except for grammar [Art VII, sec 12] Provision in subsection (4) for reconvening to consider vetoed bills is new [Subsection (5), see 1889 constitution Art VII, sec 13]

Cross-References

Bills, governor s approval or veto see 43-501 et seq

Section 11. Special session. Whenever the governor considers it in the public interest, he may convene the legislature

Convention Notes

Revises 1889 constitution [Art VII, sec 11] Continues power of governor to call

special sessions of the legislature but removes his power to limit subjects to be considered

Section 12. Pardons. The governor may grant reprieves, commutations and pardons, restore citizenship, and suspend and remit fines and forfeitures subject to procedures provided by law

Convention Notes

Revises 1889 constitution [Art VII, sec 9]. Deletes reference to board of pardons (which is provided for by law) and to the board of prison commissioners (which is defunct)

Cross-References

Probation, parole and executive clemency act see 94-9821 et seq.

Section 13   Militia   (1)   The governor is commander-in-chief of the militia forces of the state, except when they are in the actual service of the United States   He may call out any part or all of the forces to aid in the execution of the laws, suppress insurrection, repel invasion, or protect life and property in natural disasters

(2)   The militia forces shall consist of all able-bodied citizens of the state except those exempted by law.

Convention Notes

Last phrase of subsection (1) [Art VII, see 6] regarding protection of life and property is new   Subsection (2) [Art XIV, see 1] removes sex and age qualifications for militia

Cross-References

Militia, governor as commander-in chief, sec 77 103
Militia, governor's power to order out militia, secs 77-107 et seq , 94 5303 et seq

Section 14. Succession. (1)   If the governor-elect is disqualified or dies the lieutenant governor-elect upon qualifying for the office shall become governor for the full term   If the governor-elect fails to assume office for any other reason, the lieutenant governor-elect upon qualifying as such shall serve as acting governor until the governor-elect is able to assume office, or until the office, becomes vacant

(2)   The lieutenant governor shall serve as acting governor when so requested in writing by the governor   After the governor has been absent from the state for more than 45 consecutive days, the lieutenant governor shall serve as acting governor

(3)   He shall serve as acting governor when the governor is so disabled as to be unable to communicate to the lieutenant governor the fact of his inability to perform the duties of his office   The lieutenant governor shall continue to serve as acting governor until the governor is able to resume the duties of his office

(4)   Whenever, at any other time, the lieutenant governor and attorney general transmit to the legislature their written declaration that the governor is unable to discharge the powers and duties of his office, the legislature shall convene to determine whether he is able to do so

(5)   If the legislature, within 21 days after convening, determines by two-thirds vote of its members that the governor is unable to discharge the powers and duties of his office, the lieutenant governor shall serve as acting governor   Thereafter, when the governor transmits to the legislature his written declaration that no inability exists, he shall resume the powers and duties of his office within 15 days, unless the legislature determines otherwise by two-thirds vote of its members   If the legislature so determines, the lieutenant governor shall continue to serve as acting governor

(6)   If the office of governor becomes vacant by reason of death, resignation, or disqualification, the lieutenant governor shall become governor for the remainder of the term, except as provided in this constitution

22

(7) Additional succession to fill vacancies shall be provided by law

(8) When there is a vacancy in the office of governor, the successor shall be the governor. The acting governor shall have the powers and duties of the office of governor only for the period during which he serves.

Convention Notes

New provision based on 25th amendment to US Constitution If governor dies, is disqualified, or resigns, the lieutenant governor takes his place It governor is gone from the state more than 45 days or is temporarily disabled the lieutenant governor becomes acting governor If the lieutenant governor and the attorney general think the governor is unable to perform his duties they may send notice to the legislature By a two-thirds vote the legislature can decide that the lieutenant governor shall serve as acting governor because the governor is unable to act [See 1889 constitution Art VII, secs 14, 15, 16]

Section 15 Information for governor. (1) The governor may require information in writing, under oath when required, from the officers of the executive branch upon any subject relating to the duties of their respective offices

(2) He may require information in writing, under oath, from all officers and managers of state institutions

(3) He may appoint a committee to investigate and report to him upon the condition of any executive office or state institution

Convention Notes

No change except in grammar [Art VII, sec 10].

Cross-References

Annual reports to governor, secs. 82-1001, 82-1002

ARTICLE VII

THE JUDICIARY

Section 1. Judicial power. The judicial power of the state is vested in one supreme court, district courts, justice courts, and such other courts as may be provided by law.

Convention Notes

Revises 1889 constitution [Art. VIII, sec 1] by allowing the legislature to establish "inferior" courts, such as a small claims court, as well as intermediate courts of appeal Reference in 1889 constitution to senate as court of impeachment is deleted

Cross-References

Courts of state, sec 93-101
Municipal courts, sec. 11-1701 et seq
Police courts, sec 11-1601 et seq

Section 2 Supreme court jurisdiction (1) The supreme court has appellate jurisdiction and may issue, hear, and determine writs appropriate thereto It has original jurisdiction to issue, hear, and determine writs of habeas corpus and such other writs as may be provided by law

(2) It has general supervisory control over all other courts

(3) It may make rules governing appellate procedure, practice and procedure for all other courts, admission to the bar and the conduct of its

23

members Rules of procedure shall be subject to disapproval by the legislature in either of the two sessions following promulgation

(4) Supreme court process shall extend to all parts of the state

Convention Notes

(1) No change except in grammar [Art VIII, secs 2, 3] (2) No change except in grammar [Art VIII, see 2] (3) Allows Supreme Court to make rules governing itself, other courts and lawyers Legisla

ture may veto the rules (4) No change except in grammar [Art VIII, see 2]

Cross References

Jurisdiction of supreme court, see 93 213 et seq

Section 3 Supreme court organization (1) The supreme court consists of one chief justice and four justices, but the legislature may increase the number of justices from four to six A majority shall join in and pronounce decisions, which must be in writing

(2) A district judge shall be substituted for the chief justice or a justice in the event of disqualification or disability, and the opinion of the district judge sitting with the supreme court shall have the same effect as an opinion of a justice

Convention Notes

Only change, except in grammar, allows legislature to increase number of justices to six should the need arise [Art VIII, sec 5]

Cross-References

Concurrence of majority, see 93 217

Section 4. District court jurisdiction. (1) The district court has original jurisdiction in all criminal cases amounting to felony and all civil matters and cases at law and in equity It may issue all writs appropriate to its jurisdiction It shall have the power of naturalization and such additional jurisdiction as may be delegated by the laws of the United States or the state of Montana Its process shall extend to all parts of the state

(2) The district court shall hear appeals from inferior courts as trials anew unless otherwise provided by law The legislature may provide for direct review by the district court of decisions of administrative agencies

(3) Other courts may have jurisdiction of criminal cases not amounting to felony and such jurisdiction concurrent with that of the district court as may be provided by law

Convention Notes

(1) No change except in grammar [Art VIII, see 11] (2) New provision providing for appeal from lower courts and state agencies (3) New provision which allows

legislature to create other courts having the same power as district courts

Cross-References

Jurisdiction of district court, see 93-317 et seq

Section 5 Justices of the peace. (1) There shall be elected in each county at least one justice of the peace with qualifications, training, and monthly compensation provided by law There shall be provided such facilities that they may perform their duties in dignified surroundings

(2) Justice courts shall have such original jurisdiction as may be provided by law They shall not have trial jurisdiction in any criminal case designated a felony except as examining courts

(3) The legislature may provide for additional justices of the peace in each county

Convention Notes

(1) Revises 1889 constitution [Art VIII, sec 20] by requiring one justice of the peace in each county instead of two in each township and allows legislature to set qualifications, training standards and salaries Provision for "dignified surroundings" is new (2) Deletes references in 1889 constitution [Art. VIII, sec 21] to types of cases which may not be handled by a justice of the peace and provides that legislature may determine this except that they may not try felony cases (3) No change except in grammar [Art VIII, sec 20]

Cross-References

Jurisdiction of justice courts, sec 93-408 et seq

Section 6. Judicial districts. (1) The legislature shall divide the state into judicial districts and provide for the number of judges in each district Each district shall be formed of compact territory and be bounded by county lines

(2) The legislature may change the number and boundaries of judicial districts and the number of judges in each district, but no change in boundaries or the number of districts or judges therein shall work a removal of any judge from office during the term for which he was elected or appointed

(3) The chief justice may, upon request of the district judge, assign district judges and other judges for temporary service from one district to another, and from one county to another

Convention Notes

(1) (2) No change except in grammar [Art VIII, secs 12, 14] (3) New provision allowing the chief justice temporarily to assign judges to districts other than their own

Cross-References

Judicial districts, sec 93 301 et seq

Section 7. Terms and pay. (1) All justices and judges shall be paid as provided by law, but salaries shall not be diminished during terms of office

(2) Terms of office shall be eight years for supreme court justices, six years for district court judges, four years for justices of the peace, and as provided by law for other judges

Compiler's Notes

Section 4 of the Transition Schedule provides "Supreme court justices, district court judges, and justices of the peace holding office when this Constitution becomes effective shall serve the terms for which they were elected or appointed "

Convention Notes

(1) No change except in grammar [Art VIII, sec 29] (2) Supreme Court justice terms increased from six to eight years, district court judges from four to six and justices of the peace from two to four years [Art VIII, secs. 7, 12, 20]

Cross-References

District court judges, salary, sec 93 303
Justices of the peace, fees and salaries, sec 25-301 et seq
Supreme court chief justice and justices, salaries, sec 25 501.

Section 8. Selection. (1) The governor shall nominate a replacement from nominees selected in the manner provided by law for any vacancy in the office of supreme court justice or district court judge If the governor fails to nominate within thirty days after receipt of nominees, the

25

chief justice or acting chief justice shall make the nomination Each nomination shall be confirmed by the senate, but a nomination made while the senate is not in session shall be effective as an appointment until the end of the next session If the nomination is not confirmed, the office shall be vacant and another selection and nomination shall be made

(2) If, at the first election after senate confirmation, and at the election before each succeeding term of office, any candidate other than the incumbent justice or district judge files for election to that office, the name of the incumbent shall be placed on the ballot If there is no election contest for the office, the name of the incumbent shall nevertheless be placed on the general election ballot to allow voters of the state or district to approve or reject him If an incumbent is rejected, another selection and nomination shall be made

(3) If an incumbent does not run, there shall be an election for the office

Convention Notes

Revises 1889 constitution [Art VIII, secs 6, 8, 12] Contested election of judges is not changed, however if a judge in office does not have an opponent in an election his name will be put on the ballot anyway and the people asked to approve or reject him If rejected, the governor appoints another judge When there is a vacancy (such as death or resignation) the governor appoints a replacement but does not have unlimited choice of lawyers as under 1889 constitution [Art VIII sec 34] He must choose his appointee from a list of nominees and the appointment must be confirmed by the senate—a new requirement

Section 9. Qualifications. (1) A citizen of the United States who has resided in the state two years immediately before taking office is eligible to the office of supreme court justice or district court judge if admitted to the practice of law in Montana for at least five years prior to the date of appointment or election Qualifications and methods of selection of judges of other courts shall be provided by law

(2) No supreme court justice or district court judge shall solicit or receive compensation in any form whatever on account of his office, except salary and actual necessary travel expense

(3) Except as otherwise provided in this constitution, no supreme court justice or district court judge shall practice law during his term of office, engage in any other employment for which salary or fee is paid, or hold office in a political party.

(4) Supreme court justices shall reside within the state Every other judge shall reside during his term of office in the district, county, township, precinct, city or town in which he is elected or appointed

Convention Notes

(1) Revises 1889 constitution [Art VIII, secs 10, 16] by making residency requirements for candidates for district court judgeship the same as for supreme court and by deleting age requirements Requirement for five years of law practice new (2) Revises 1889 constitution [Art VIII, sec 30] by specifically allowing travel expense (3) Only change [Art VIII, sec 35] specifically prohibits a judge from holding office in a political party (4) No change except in grammar [Art VIII, sec 33]

Cross-References

Qualifications and residence of judicial officers, sec 93-701 et seq

Section 10   Forfeiture of judicial position Any holder of a judicial position forfeits that position by either filing for an elective public office other than a judicial position or absenting himself from the state for more than 60 consecutive days

Convention Notes

New provision A judge may not run for any other public office, or be out of state for more than 60 days [See 1889 constitution Art VIII, see 37]

Section 11.   Removal and discipline. (1) The legislature shall create a judicial standards commission consisting of five persons and provide for the appointment thereto of two district judges, one attorney, and two citizens who are neither judges nor attorneys

(2) The commission shall investigate complaints, make rules implementing this section, and keep its proceedings confidential It may subpoena witnesses and documents

(3) Upon recommendation of the commission, the supreme court may

(a) Retire any justice or judge for disability that seriously interferes with the performance of his duties and is or may become permanent, or

(b) Censure, suspend, or remove any justice or judge for willful misconduct in office, willful and persistent failure to perform his duties, or habitual intemperance

Convention Notes

New provision A judicial standards commission may investigate whenever a judge, because of disability or bad habits, does not perform his duties properly The commission can recommend to the supreme court that the judge be retired, censured suspended or removed

ARTICLE VIII

REVENUE AND FINANCE

Section 1   Tax purposes Taxes shall be levied by general laws for public purposes

Convention Notes

Revises 1889 constitution [Art XII] by eliminating references to particular kinds of revenue sources (such as property taxes license fees, and income taxes) and continues the legislative power to determine tax structures

Section 2.   Tax power inalienable The power to tax shall never be surrendered, suspended, or contracted away

Convention Notes

New section which limits the power to tax to government

Section 3   Property tax administration. The state shall appraise, assess, and equalize the valuation of all property which is to be taxed in the manner provided by law

Convention Notes

Revises 1889 constitution [Art XII, see 15] by removing references to county boards of equalization and state board of equalization leaving the legislature free to determine the method of securing property tax equalization

Cross-References

Classification of property for taxation, sec 84-301

Section 4   Equal valuation All taxing jurisdictions shall use the assessed valuation of property established by the state

Convention Notes
No change except in grammar [Art XII, sec 5] Guarantees the same assessed

value will be used by all taxing authorities

Section 5   Property tax exemptions. (1) The legislature may exempt from taxation

(a) Property of the United States, the state, counties, cities, towns, school districts, municipal corporations, and public libraries, but any private interest in such property may be taxed separately

(b) Institutions of purely public charity, hospitals and places of burial not used or held for private or corporate profit, places for actual religious worship, and property used exclusively for educational purposes

(c) Any other classes of property

(2) The legislature may authorize creation of special improvement districts for capital improvements and the maintenance thereof It may authorize the assessment of charges for such improvements and maintenance against tax exempt property directly benefited thereby

Convention Notes
1889 constitution [Art XII, sec 2] makes it mandatory that all property listed in subsection (1) (a) be exempt from taxation Revision leaves all exemptions at discretion of legislature Specifically permits taxation of private interests

in government-owned property and assessment of special improvement district charges on tax exempt property

Cross-References
Exemptions from taxation, see 84-202

Section 6   Highway revenue non-diversion. (1) Revenue from gross vehicle weight fees and excise and license taxes (except general sales and use taxes) on gasoline, fuel, and other energy sources used to propel vehicles on public highways shall be used as authorized by the legislature, after deduction of statutory refunds and adjustments, solely for

(a) Payment of obligations incurred for construction, reconstruction, repair, operation, and maintenance of public highways, streets, roads, and bridges

(b) Payment of county, city, and town obligations on streets, roads, and bridges

(c) Enforcement of highway safety, driver education, tourist promotion, and administrative collection costs

(2) Such revenue may be appropriated for other purposes by a three-fifths vote of the members of each house of the legislature

Convention Notes
Revises 1956 amendment to the 1889 constitution [Art XII, sec 1b] by removing motor vehicle registration fees from the earmarking provision, by including local government road and street

systems, highway safety programs and driver education programs is permissible uses of earmarked funds, and by allowing the legislature by a three fifths vote to divert the earmarked funds to other purposes

Section 7.   Tax appeals. The legislature shall provide independent appeal procedures for taxpayer grievances about appraisals, assessments, equalization, and taxes The legislature shall include a review procedure at the local government unit level

Convention Notes

New provision requiring the legislature to establish procedures for taxpayer appeals Appeal procedures must include an opportunity to have the complaint heard at the local level

Section 8 State debt No state debt shall be created unless authorized by a two-thirds vote of the members of each house of the legislature or a majority of the electors voting thereon No state debt shall be created to cover deficits incurred because appropriations exceeded anticipated revenue

Convention Notes

Revises 1889 constitution [Art XIII, sec 2] by replacing obsolete $100,000 limit on state debt with provision that only a 2/3 vote of the legislature or majority vote at an election may create state debt

Section 9 Balanced budget Appropriations by the legislature shall not exceed anticipated revenue

Convention Notes

No change except in grammar [Art XII, sec 12] Requires legislature to stay within estimated revenue limits when appropriating funds

Section 10. Local government debt The legislature shall by law limit debts of counties, cities, towns, and all other local governmental entities.

Convention Notes

Revises 1889 constitution [Art XIII, secs 5, 6] Debt limitations for all local governmental entities will be set by law rather than by the constitution

Cross-References

County indebtedness, limit, sec 16-807
Municipal indebtedness, limit, secs 11-966, 11-2303.

Section 11. Use of loan proceeds. All money borrowed by or on behalf of the state or any county, city, town, or other local governmental entity shall be used only for purposes specified in the authorizing law

Convention Notes

No change except in grammar [Art XIII, sec 3]

Section 12 Strict accountability. The legislature shall by law insure strict accountability of all revenue received and money spent by the state and counties, cities, towns, and all other local governmental entities

Convention Notes

Revises 1889 constitution [Art XII, sec 13] by leaving specific details of accounting procedures, reporting requirements, etc to the legislature

Section 13 Investment of public funds. (1) The legislature shall provide for a unified investment program for public funds and provide rules therefor, including supervision of investment of surplus funds of all counties, cities, towns, and other local governmental entities Each fund forming a part of the unified investment program shall be separately identified Except for monies contributed to retirement funds, no public funds shall be invested in private corporate capital stock The investment program shall be audited at least annually and a report thereof submitted to the governor and legislature

(2) The public school fund and the permanent funds of the Montana university system and all other state institutions of learning shall be safely and conservatively invested in

(a) Public securities of the state, its subdivisions, local government units, and districts within the state, or

(b) Bonds of the United States or other securities fully guaranteed as to principal and interest by the United States, or

(c) Such other safe investments bearing a fixed rate of interest as may be provided by law

Convention Notes

Revises 1889 constitution [Art XXI] by providing for a unified investment program for all state funds Allows retirement funds to be invested in private corporate stock, but provides that the public school fund and university system funds may be invested only in interest bearing securities

Cross-References

Bond of investments, creation, transfer of investment functions sees 82A-204, 82A 205

Section 14. Prohibited payments Except for interest on the public debt, no money shall be paid out of the treasury unless upon an appropriation made by law and a warrant drawn by the proper officer in pursuance thereof

Convention Notes

No change except in grammar [Art XII, see 10]

ARTICLE IX

ENVIRONMENT AND NATURAL RESOURCES

Section 1   Protection and improvement. (1) The state and each person shall maintain and improve a clean and healthful environment in Montana for present and future generations

(2) The legislature shall provide for the administration and enforcement of this duty

(3) The legislature shall provide adequate remedies for the protection of the environmental life support system from degradation and provide adequate remedies to prevent unreasonable depletion and degradation of natural resources

Convention Notes

New provision creating a duty of the state and its people to protect and improve the environment

Cross References

Environmental Policy Act, sees 69-6501 et seq

Fish and game department, creation, see 82A-2001.

Health and environmental sciences, department created, see 82A-601

Natural resources and conservation, department created, see 82A-1501

State lands, department created, see 82A-1101

Section 2. Reclamation. All lands disturbed by the taking of natural resources shall be reclaimed The legislature shall provide effective requirements and standards for the reclamation of lands disturbed

Convention Notes

New provision requiring restoration of land after removal of natural resources

Section 3   Water rights   (1) All existing rights to the use of any waters for any useful or beneficial purpose are hereby recognized and confirmed

(2)   The use of all water that is now or may hereafter be appropriated for sale, rent, distribution, or other beneficial use, the right of way over the lands of others for all ditches, drains, flumes, canals and aqueducts necessarily used in connection therewith, and the sites for reservoirs necessary for collecting and storing water shall be held to be a public use

(3)   All surface, underground, flood, and atmospheric waters within the boundaries of the state are the property of the state for the use of its people and are subject to appropriation for beneficial uses as provided by law

(4)   The legislature shall provide for the administration, control, and regulation of water rights and shall establish a system of centralized records, in addition to the present system of local records

Convention Notes

(1) New provision guaranteeing all existing rights to the use of water (2) No change except in grammar [Art III, see 15] (3) New provision recognizing state ownership of all water subject to use and appropriation by its people (4) New provision requiring legislature to pass laws establishing a central records system so that records of water rights may be found in a single location as well as locally

Section 4   Cultural resources   The legislature shall provide for the identification, acquisition, restoration, enhancement, preservation, and administration of scenic, historic, archeologic, scientific, cultural, and recreational areas, sites, records and objects, and for their use and enjoyment by the people

Convention Notes

New provision Self explanatory

ARTICLE X

EDUCATION AND PUBLIC LANDS

Section 1. Educational goals and duties   (1) It is the goal of the people to establish a system of education which will develop the full educational potential of each person Equality of educational opportunity is guaranteed to each person of the state

(2)   The state recognizes the distinct and unique cultural heritage of the American Indians and is committed in its educational goals to the preservation of their cultural integrity

(3)   The legislature shall provide a basic system of free quality public elementary and secondary schools The legislature may provide such other educational institutions, public libraries, and educational programs as it deems desirable It shall fund and distribute in an equitable manner to the school districts the state's share of the cost of the basic elementary and secondary school system

Convention Notes

Revises 1889 Constitution [Art XI, secs 1, 6, 7] Expresses the goal of the State to educate all of its citizens regardless of their ages Creates a right to equal educational opportunity and specifically recognizes unique heritage of Indians

Section 2. Public school fund. The public school fund of the state shall consist of (1) Proceeds from the school lands which have been or may hereafter be granted by the United States,

(2)   Lands granted in lieu thereof,

(3)   Lands given or granted by any person or corporation under any law or grant of the United States,

(4)   All other grants of land or money made from the United States for general educational purposes or without special purpose,

(5)   All interests in estates that escheat to the state,

(6)   All unclaimed shares and dividends of any corporation incorporated in the state,

(7)   All other grants, gifts, devises or bequests made to the state for general educational purposes

Convention Notes

No change except in grammar [Art XI, sec 2] Gives constitutional recognition to the public school fund

Cross-References

Public school fund, see 75 7301 et seq

Section 3   Public school fund inviolate   The public school fund shall forever remain inviolate guaranteed by the state against loss or diversion

Convention Notes

No change except in grammar [Art XI, sec 3]

Section 4. Board of land commissioners   The governor, superintendent of public instruction, auditor, secretary of state and attorney general constitute the board of land commissioners It has the authority to direct, control, lease, exchange and sell school lands and lands which have been or may be granted for the support and benefit of the various state educational institutions, under such regulations and restrictions as may be provided by law

Convention Notes

Revises 1889 constitution [Art XI, sec 4] by adding state auditor to board of land commissioners and adding the power to exchange lands

Cross-References

Composition of board of land commissioners, see 82-904

Powers and duties of board of land commissioners, see 81-103

Section 5. Public school fund revenue. (1) Ninety-five percent of all the interest received on the public school fund and ninety-five percent of all rent received from the leasing of school lands and all other income

32

from the public school fund shall be equitably apportioned annually to public elementary and secondary school districts as provided by law

(2) The remaining five percent of all interest received on the public school fund, and the remaining five percent of all rent received from the leasing of school lands and all other income from the public school fund shall annually be added to the public school fund and become and forever remain an inseparable and inviolable part thereof

Convention Notes

Revises 1889 constitution [Art XI, sec 5] by replacing specific language requiring distribution to be made "in proportion to the number of children between ages of 6 and 21" with general language that the income be "equitably apportioned"

and by allowing distribution of interest and income moneys to high schools as well as elementary schools

Cross-References

Apportionment from fund, see 75-6908 et seq

Section 6 Aid prohibited to sectarian schools. (1) The legislature, counties, cities, towns, school districts, and public corporations shall not make any direct or indirect appropriation or payment from any public fund or monies, or any grant of lands or other property for any sectarian purpose or to aid any church, school, academy, seminary, college, university, or other literary or scientific institution, controlled in whole or in part by any church, sect, or denomination

(2) This section shall not apply to funds from federal sources provided to the state for the express purpose of distribution to non-public education

Convention Notes

Revises 1889 constitution [Art XI sec 8] by specifying that federal funds may

be distributed to private schools Proposed section still prohibits state aid to private schools

Section 7. Non-discrimination in education No religious or partisan test or qualification shall be required of any teacher or student as a condition of admission into any public educational institution Attendance shall not be required at any religious service No sectarian tenets shall be advocated in any public educational institution of the state No person shall be refused admission to any public educational institution on account of sex, race, creed, religion, political beliefs, or national origin

Convention Notes

Last sentence revises 1889 constitution [Art XI, sec 9] (which merely forbade denying any person entrance to a university because of his or her sex) by broaden

ing the language to include all public educational institutions and to include other kinds of discrimination Other changes in grammar only

Section 8 School district trustees The supervision and control of schools in each school district shall be vested in a board of trustees to be elected as provided by law

Convention Notes

New provision which guarantees control of schools to local boards Deletes requirement in 1889 constitution [Art XI, sec 10] that elections for school dis

trict officers must be separate from state and county elections

Cross References

School district trustees, see 75-5901 et seq

Section 9   Boards of education. (1) There is a state board of education composed of the board of regents of higher education and the board of public education It is responsible for long-range planning, and for coordinating and evaluating policies and programs for the state's educational systems It shall submit unified budget requests A tie vote at any meeting may be broken by the governor, who is an ex officio member of each component board

(2) (a) The government and control of the Montana university system is vested in a board of regents of higher education which shall have full power, responsibility, and authority to supervise, coordinate, manage and control the Montana university system and shall supervise and coordinate other public educational institutions assigned by law

(b) The board consists of seven members appointed by the governor, and confirmed by the senate, to overlapping terms, as provided by law The governor and superintendent of public instruction are ex officio nonvoting members of the board

(c) The board shall appoint a commissioner of higher education and prescribe his term and duties

(d) The funds and appropriations under the control of the board of regents are subject to the same audit provisions as are all other state funds

(3) (a) There is a board of public education to exercise general supervision over the public school system and such other public educational institutions as may be assigned by law Other duties of the board shall be provided by law.

(b) The board consists of seven members appointed by the governor, and confirmed by the senate, to overlapping terms as provided by law The governor, commissioner of higher education and state superintendent of public instruction shall be ex officio non-voting members of the board

Section 10   State university funds The funds of the Montana university system and of all other state institutions of learning, from whatever source accruing, shall forever remain inviolate and sacred to the purpose for which they were dedicated The various funds shall be respectively invested under such regulations as may be provided by law, and shall be guaranteed by the state against loss or diversion The interest from such invested funds, together with the rent from leased lands or properties, shall be devoted to the maintenance and perpetuation of the respective institutions

Convention Notes
No change except in grammar [Art XI, sec 12] (Section 13 of Article VIII,

REVENUE AND FINANCE provides for the investment of university funds)

Section 11. Public land trust, disposition. (1) All lands of the state that have been or may be granted by congress, or acquired by gift or grant or devise from any person or corporation, shall be public lands of the state They shall be held in trust for the people, to be disposed of as hereafter provided, for the respective purposes for which they have been or may be granted, donated or devised

(2) No such land or any estate or interest therein shall ever be disposed of except in pursuance of general laws providing for such disposition, or until the full market value of the estate or interest disposed of, to be ascertained in such manner as may be provided by law, has been paid or safely secured to the state.

(3) No land which the state holds by grant from the United States which prescribes the manner of disposal and minimum price shall be disposed of except in the manner and for at least the price prescribed without the consent of the United States

(4) All public land shall be classified by the board of land commissioners in a manner provided by law Any public land may be exchanged for other land, public or private, which is equal in value and, as closely as possible, equal in area

Convention Notes
Only change in subsections (1), (2) and (3) are in grammar. Subsection (4) revises 1889 constitution by deleting the 1889 constitutional classification of prop-

erty into grazing, timber agricultural or city lands and by stipulating that public lands may be exchanged [Art XVII, secs 1, 2, 3]

ARTICLE XI

LOCAL GOVERNMENT

Section 1 Definition The term 'local government units' includes, but is not limited to, counties and incorporated cities and towns Other local government units may be established by law

Convention Notes
New provision defining the term "local government unit" to include counties, cities and towns

Section 2 Counties. The counties of the state are those that exist on the date of ratification of this constitution No county boundary may be changed or county seat transferred until approved by a majority of those voting on the question in each county affected

Convention Notes
Revises 1889 constitution [Art XVI, sec 2] by requiring only majority of those voting to approve county seat or boundary changes 1889 constitution requires ma-

jority of qualified electors [See also 1889 constitution Art XVI, sec 1]

Cross-References
County boundaries, see 16 201 et seq
Removal of county seat, see 16 301 et seq

Section 3. Forms of government (1) The legislature shall provide methods for governing local government units and procedures for incorporating, classifying, merging, consolidating, and dissolving such units, and altering their boundaries The legislature shall provide such optional or alternative forms of government that each unit or combination of units may adopt, amend, or abandon an optional or alternative form by a majority of those voting on the question

(2) One optional form of county government includes, but is not limited to, the election of three county commissioners, a clerk and recorder, a clerk of district court, a county attorney, a sheriff, a treasurer, a surveyor, a county superintendent of schools, an assessor, a coroner, and a public administrator The terms, qualifications, duties, and compensation of those offices shall be provided by law The Board of county commissioners may consolidate two or more such offices The Boards of two or more counties may provide for a joint office and for the election of one official to perform the duties of any such office in those counties

Convention Notes

New provision directing legislature to provide alternative forms of city and county or city county governments, one of which must be the "traditional" form including the elected officials listed Two or more counties may agree to elect one official to serve a multicounty area Offices within counties are subject to consolidation [See Art XVI, secs 4, 5, 6, 7, 8]

Section 4. General powers. (1) A local government unit without self-government powers has the following general powers

(a) An incorporated city or town has the powers of a municipal corporation and legislative, administrative, and other powers provided or implied by law

(b) A county has legislative, administrative, and other powers provided or implied by law

(c) Other local government units have powers provided by law

(2) The powers of incorporated cities and towns and counties shall be liberally construed

Convention Notes

New provision allowing legislature to grant legislative, administrative and other powers to local government units

Section 5 Self-government charters (1) The legislature shall provide procedures permitting a local government unit or combination of units to frame, adopt, amend, revise, or abandon a self-government charter with the approval of a majority of those voting on the question The procedures shall not require approval of a charter by a legislative body

(2) If the legislature does not provide such procedures by July 1, 1975, they may be established by election either

(a) Initiated by petition in the local government unit or combination of units, or

(b) Called by the governing body of the local government unit or combination of units.

(3) Charter provisions establishing executive, legislative, and administrative structure and organization are superior to statutory provisions

Convention Notes

New provision directing legislature to pass laws concerning procedures for local voters to design their own forms of gov-

ernment (self-government charters) The charter provisions concerning structure of local governments would take precedence over general laws on such matters

Section 6 Self-government powers A local government unit adopting a self-government charter may exercise any power not prohibited by this constitution, law, or charter This grant of self-government powers may be extended to other local government units through optional forms of government provided for in section 3

Convention Notes

New provision allowing local government units to share powers with the state

and to have all powers not specifically denied At present local governments have only those powers specifically granted

Section 7 Intergovernmental cooperation (1) Unless prohibited by law or charter, a local government unit may

(a) cooperate in the exercise of any function, power, or responsibility with,

(b) share the services of any officer or facilities with,

(c) transfer or delegate any function, power, responsibility, or duty of any officer to one or more other local government units, school districts, the state, or the United States

(2) The qualified electors of a local government unit may, by initiative or referendum, require it to do so

Convention Notes

New provision allowing local governments to share services and functions

with other units of government, the state and the United States

Section 8 Initiative and referendum The legislature shall extend the initiative and referendum powers reserved to the people by the constitution to the qualified electors of each local government unit

Convention Notes

New provision directing legislature to give residents the power to initiate local ordinances by petition or to petition to vote on ordinances passed by local governments

Cross-References

Reservation of powers of initiative and referendum, Const Art V, sec 1

Section 9 Voter review of local government. (1) The legislature shall, within four years of the ratification of this constitution, provide procedures requiring each local government unit or combination of units to review its structure and submit one alternative form of government to the qualified electors at the next general or special election

(2) The legislature shall require a review procedure once every ten years after the first election

Convention Notes

New provision By 1976 the legislature must give local residents the opportunity to vote on whether or not to change their

form of government Laws must be passed requiring local forms of government to be studied and evaluated every ten years

ARTICLE XII

DEPARTMENTS AND INSTITUTIONS

Section 1. Agriculture (1) The legislature shall provide for a Department of Agriculture and enact laws and provide appropriations to protect, enhance, and develop all agriculture.

(2) Special levies may be made on livestock and on agricultural commodities for disease control and indemnification predator control, and livestock and commodity inspection, protection, research, and promotion Revenue derived shall be used solely for the purposes of the levies

Convention Notes

(1) Revises 1889 constitution [Art XVIII, sec 1] Provides that a department of agriculture will be one of the 20 departments in the executive branch Deletes reference to a commissioner of agriculture Directs legislature to provide money for agriculture (2) Revises 1889 constitution [Art XII, sec 9] by extend ing the special mill levy on livestock to agriculture to be used for the benefit of both Deletes reference to maximum levy allowed

Cross-References

Department of agriculture, creation, see 82A-301.

Section 2. Labor. (1) The legislature shall provide for a Department of Labor and Industry, headed by a Commissioner appointed by the governor and confirmed by the senate

(2) A maximum period of 8 hours is a regular day's work in all industries and employment except agriculture and stock raising The legislature may change this maximum period to promote the general welfare

Convention Notes

2 No change except in grammar [Art XVIII, secs 1, 4] Provides that department of labor will be one of the 20 departments in the executive branch

Cross-References

Department of labor and industry, creation, commissioner, sec. 82A-1001.

Section 3. Institutions and assistance (1) The state shall establish and support institutions and facilities as the public good may require, including homes which may be necessary and desirable for the care of veterans

(2) Persons committed to any such institutions shall retain all rights except those necessarily suspended as a condition of commitment Suspended rights are restored upon termination of the state's responsibility

(3) The legislature shall provide such economic assistance and social and rehabilitative services as may be necessary for those inhabitants who, by reason of age, infirmities, or misfortune may have need for the aid of society

Convention Notes

(1) No change except in grammar [Art X, sec 1] (Deletes references to specific types of institutions) (2) New provision that a person in an institution may exercise all rights except those that are impossible because of the confinement and that all rights are automatically restored when the person is released (3) Revises 1889 constitution [Art X, sec 5] which states that the "several counties" must provide welfare Revision leaves it up to the legislature to determine whether the state, county or a combination of the two must provide welfare

ARTICLE XIII

GENERAL PROVISIONS

Section 1. Non-municipal corporations (1) Corporate charters shall be granted, modified, or dissolved only pursuant to general law

(2) The legislature shall provide protection and education for the people against harmful and unfair practices by either foreign or domestic corporations, individuals, or associations

(3) The legislature shall pass no law retrospective in its operations which imposes on the people a new liability in respect to transactions or considerations already passed

Convention Notes

(1) No change except in grammar [Art XV sec 2] (2) New provision requiring the legislature to pass consumer protection laws (3) New provision prohibiting laws which would add liabilities to past contracts

Cross-References

Corporations, Title 15

Section 2 Consumer counsel The legislature shall provide for an office of consumer counsel which shall have the duty of representing consumer interests in hearings before the public service commission or any other successor agency The legislature shall provide for the funding of the office of consumer counsel by a special tax on the net income or gross revenues of regulated companies

Convention Notes

New provision requiring legislature to create a state office to represent customers at hearings before the public service commission Utility companies would be taxed to support the office

Section 3 Salary commission The legislature shall create a salary commission to recommend compensation for the judiciary and elected members of the legislative and executive branches

Convention Notes

New provision requiring legislature to create a committee which would suggest salary schedules for judges, legislators and executive officials

Section 4 Code of ethics The legislature shall provide a code of ethics prohibiting conflict between public duty and private interest for members of the legislature and all state and local officers and employees

Convention Notes

New provision The legislature must enact laws concerning conflict of interest involving legislators and other public officials

Section 5 Exemption laws The legislature shall enact liberal homestead and exemption laws

Convention Notes

Identical to 1889 Constitution [Art XIX, sec 4].

Cross-References

Earnings exempt from execution, sec 93 5816 et seq
Homesteads, sec 33 101 et seq
Property exempt from execution, sec 93 5813 et seq

Section 6.   Perpetuities   No perpetuities shall be allowed except for charitable purposes

Convention Notes

Identical to 1889 Constitution [Art XIX, sec 5]

Cross-References

Rule against perpetuities, secs 67-406, 67-407

ARTICLE XIV

CONSTITUTIONAL REVISION

Section 1   Constitutional convention.   The legislature, by an affirmative vote of two-thirds of all the members, whether one or more bodies, may at any time submit to the qualified electors the question of whether there shall be an unlimited convention to revise, alter, or amend this constitution

Convention Notes

Adds word "unlimited" to 1889 constitution [Art XIX, sec 8] Makes it clear that the legislature cannot call a constitutional convention for limited purpose.

Section 2   Initiative for constitutional convention   (1) The people may by initiative petition direct the secretary of state to submit to the qualified electors the question of whether there shall be an unlimited convention to revise, alter, or amend this constitution The petition shall be signed by at least ten percent of the qualified electors of the state That number shall include at least ten percent of the qualified electors in each of two-fifths of the legislative districts

(2)   The secretary of state shall certify the filing of the petition in his office and cause the question to be submitted at the next general election

Convention Notes

New provision Enables people to petition to call a constitutional convention

Cross-References

Initiative and referendum provisions of Article III not applicable to constitutional revision, Const Art III, sec 8

Section 3   Periodic submission   If the question of holding a convention is not otherwise submitted during any period of 20 years, it shall be submitted as provided by law at the general election in the twentieth year following the last submission

Convention Notes

New provision The question of holding a constitutional convention must be submitted to vote of the people at least once every 20 years

Section 4.   Call of convention.   If a majority of those voting on the question answer in the affirmative, the legislature shall provide for the calling thereof at its next session The number of delegates to the convention shall be the same as that of the larger body of the legislature The qualifications of delegates shall be the same as the highest qualifications required for election to the legislature The legislature shall determine whether the delegates may be nominated on a partisan or a non-partisan basis They shall be elected at the same places and in the same districts as are the members of the legislative body determining the number of delegates.

Convention Notes

Revises 1889 constitution [Art XIX, sec 8]. Legislature shall determine whether constitutional convention delegates be elected on partisan or non partisan basis (1889 constitution not explicit on this point Montana Supreme Court held convention delegates must run on partisan basis)

Section 5. Convention expenses The legislature shall, in the act calling the convention, designate the day, hour and place of its meeting, and fix and provide for the pay of its members and officers and the necessary expenses of the convention

Convention Notes

No change except in grammar [Art XIX, sec 8]

Section 6 Oath, vacancies Before proceeding, the delegates shall take the oath provided in this constitution Vacancies occurring shall be filled in the manner provided for filling vacancies in the legislature if not otherwise provided by law.

Convention Notes

No change except in grammar [Art XIX, sec 8]

Cross-References

Oath of office, Const Art III, sec 3 Vacancies in legislature, Const Art V, sec 7

Section 7 Convention duties The convention shall meet after the election of the delegates and prepare such revisions, alterations, or amendments to the constitution as may be deemed necessary They shall be submitted to the qualified electors for ratification or rejection as a whole or in separate articles or amendments as determined by the convention at an election appointed by the convention for that purpose not less than two months after adjournment Unless so submitted and approved by a majority of the electors voting thereon, no such revision, alteration, or amendment shall take effect

Convention Notes

Only change is removal of requirements in 1889 constitution [Art XIX, sec 8] that a convention meet within a certain time after election and that the election on the proposed constitution be held within six months

Section 8 Amendment by legislative referendum. Amendments to this constitution may be proposed by any member of the legislature If adopted by an affirmative roll call vote of two-thirds of all the members thereof, whether one or more bodies, the proposed amendment shall be submitted to the qualified electors at the next general election If approved by a majority of the electors voting thereon, the amendment shall become a part of this constitution on the first day of July after certification of the election returns unless the amendment provides otherwise

Convention Notes

Revises 1889 constitution [Art XIX, sec 9] Legislature may propose constitutional amendment by a vote of two-thirds of total membership rather than two thirds of each house Provides for July effective date for amendments

41

Section 9   Amendment by initiative   (1) The people may also propose constitutional amendments by initiative. Petitions including the full text of the proposed amendment shall be signed by at least ten percent of the qualified electors of the state. That number shall include at least ten percent of the qualified electors in each of two-fifths of the legislative districts

(2) The petitions shall be filed with the secretary of state If the petitions are found to have been signed by the required number of electors, the secretary of state shall cause the amendment to be published as provided by law twice each month for two months previous to the next regular state-wide election

(3) At that election, the proposed amendment shall be submitted to the qualified electors for approval or rejection If approved by a majority voting thereon, it shall become a part of the constitution effective the first day of July following its approval, unless the amendment provides otherwise

Convention Notes

New provision Ten percent of voters may propose constitutional amendments by petition

Cross-References

Initiative and referendum provisions of Article III not applicable to constitutional revision, Const Art III, sec 8

Section 10   Petition signers   The number of qualified electors required for the filing of any petition provided for in this Article shall be determined by the number of votes cast for the office of governor in the preceding general election

Convention Notes

New provision Self explanatory

Section 11   Submission   If more than one amendment is submitted at the same election, each shall be so prepared and distinguished that it can be voted upon separately

Convention Notes

No change except in grammar [Art XIV, sec 9].

Cross-References

Attorney general's summary, sec 37-104 1
Publication and printing requirements, sec 37-107

Done in open convention at the city of Helena, in the state of Montana, this twenty-second day of March, in the year of our Lord one thousand nine hundred and seventy-two

LEO GRAYBILL, JR , PRESIDENT
JEAN M. BOWMAN, SECRETARY
MAGNUS AASHEIM
JOHN H ANDERSON, JR
OSCAR L ANDERSON
HAROLD ARBANAS
FRANKLIN ARNESS
CEDOR B ARONOW
WILLIAM H ARTZ

THOMAS M ASK
BETTY BABCOCK
LLOYD BARNARD
GRACE C BATES
DON E BELCHER
BEN E BERG, JR
E M BERTHELSON
CHET BLAYLOCK
VIRGINIA H BLEND

GEOFFREY L BRAZIER
BRUCE M. BROWN
DAPHNE BUGBEE
WILLIAM A. BURKHARDT
MARJORIE CAIN
BOB CAMPBELL
JEROME J. CATE
RICHARD J. CHAMPOUX
LYMAN W CHOATE
MAX CONOVER
C LOUISE CROSS
WADE J DAHOOD
CARL M DAVIS
DOUGLAS DELANEY
MAURICE DRISCOLL
DAVE DRUM
DOROTHY ECK
MARIAN S ERDMANN
LESLIE ESKILDSEN
MARK ETCHART
JAMES R. FELT
DONALD R FOSTER
NOEL D FURLONG
J C GARLINGTON
E S GYSLER
OTTO T. HABEDANK
GENE HARBAUGH
ROD HANSON
R S HANSON
PAUL K HARLOW
GEORGE HARPER
DANIEL W. HARRINGTON
GEORGE B HELIKER
DAVID L HOLLAND
ARNOLD W JACOBSEN
GEORGE H JAMES
TORREY B JOHNSON
THOMAS F JOYCE
A W KAMHOOT
ROBERT LEE KELLEHER
JOHN H LEUTHOLD
JEROME T LOENDORF

PETER "PETE" LORELLO
JOSEPH H McCARVEL
RUSSELL C McDONOUGH
MIKE McKEON
CHARLES B McNEIL
CHARLES H MAHONEY
RACHELL K MANSFIELD
FRED J MARTIN
J MASON MELVIN
LYLE R MONROE
MARSHALL MURRAY
ROBERT B NOBLE
RICHARD A NUTTING
MRS. THOMAS PAYNE
CATHERINE PEMBERTON
DONALD REBAL
ARLYNE E REICHERT
MRS MAE NAN ROBINSON
RICHARD B ROEDER
GEORGE W. ROLLINS
MILES ROMNEY
STERLING RYGG
DON SCANLIN
JOHN M SCHLITZ
HENRY SIDERIUS
CLARK E SIMON
CARMAN M SKARI
M LYNN SPARKS
LUCILE SPEER
R J STUDER, SR
MRS JOHN JUSTIN (VERONICA)
  SULLIVAN
WILLIAM H SWANBERG
JOHN H. TOOLE
MRS EDITH M VAN BUSKIRK
ROBERT VERMILLION
ROGER A WAGNER
JACK K WARD
MARGARET S WARDEN
ARCHIE O WILSON
ROBERT F WOODMANSEY

TRANSITION SCHEDULE

The following provisions shall remain part of this Constitution until
their terms have been executed. Once each year the attorney general shall
review the following provisions and certify to the secretary of state which,

if any, have been executed Any provisions so certified shall thereafter be removed from this Schedule and no longer published as part of this Constitution

Convention Notes

Provides for an orderly change from the 1889 constitution to the 1972 constitution

Section 1   Accelerated effective date   Section 6 (SESSIONS) and section 14 (DISTRICTING AND APPORTIONMENT) of Article V THE LEGISLATURE, shall be effective January 1, 1973

Compiler's Notes

Section 1 of the Adoption Schedule provided 'This Constitution, if approved by a majority of those voting at the election as provided by the Constitution of 1889, shall take effect on July 1, 1973, except as otherwise provided in sections 1 and 2 of the Transition Schedule The Constitution of 1889 as amended, shall thereafter be of no effect '

The Adoption Schedule, submitted with the proposed Constitution for limited purposes only, is not reprinted in this pamphlet since the introduction to the schedule provided that it should not be published is a part of the new Constitution

Convention Notes

Proposed section on annual legislative sessions and reapportionment of the legislature would be effective January 1, 1973 The reapportionment commission could then be appointed by the 1973 legislature and report its plan to the 1974 legislature

Section 2   Delayed effective date   The provisions of sections 1, 2 and 3 of Article V, THE LEGISLATURE, shall not become effective until the date the first redistricting and reapportionment plan becomes law

Convention Notes

Sections on size of legislature, election and terms of its members would become effective when the reapportionment plan becomes law If this is in 1974 then elections would be held in November 1974 for new members of the legislature to take office January 1, 1975

Section 3   Prospective operation of declaration of rights   Any rights, procedural or substantive, created for the first time by Article II shall be prospective and not retroactive

Convention Notes

Any new rights created in Article II take effect only after July 1, 1973 It does not create any rights for past events

Section 4   Terms of judiciary   Supreme court justices, district court judges and justices of the peace holding office when this Constitution becomes effective shall serve the terms for which they were elected or appointed

Convention Notes

Since the proposed constitution changes the length of terms of office of judges this provision makes it clear that all judges may serve to the end of the term for which they were elected

44

Section 5   Terms of legislators   (1) The terms of all legislators elected before the effective date of this Constitution shall end on December 31 of the year in which the first redistricting and reapportionment plan becomes law

(2) The senators first elected under this Constitution shall draw lots to establish a term of two years for one-half of their number

Convention Notes

(1) If the reapportionment and redistricting plan becomes effective after the 1974 legislative session, the terms of legislators serving in that session would end December 31, 1974 (2) Section 3, Article V provides that senators have four year terms but that one-half are elected every two years This section provides that one-half of the senators first elected will have only two year terms

Section 6   General transition   (1) The rights and duties of all public bodies shall remain as if this Constitution had not been adopted with the exception of such changes as are contained in this Constitution All laws, ordinances, regulations, and rules of court not contrary to, or inconsistent with, the provisions of this Constitution shall remain in force, until they shall expire by their own limitation or shall be altered or repealed pursuant to this Constitution

(2) The validity of all public and private bonds debts, and contracts, and of all suits, actions, and rights of action, shall continue as if no change had taken place

(3) All officers filling any office by election or appointment shall continue the duties thereof, until the end of the terms to which they were appointed or elected, and until their offices shall have been abolished or their successors selected and qualified in accordance with this Constitution or laws enacted pursuant thereto

Convention Notes

Unless the proposed constitution specifically changes a law it will not affect any rights or duties or the validity of contracts, bonds, etc All elected officials serve out their present terms

45

INDEX TO CONSTITUTION

References are Article and Section Numbers

A

Actions—See Civil actions and procedure, Crimes and criminal procedure

Acts, V, 11—See Bills

Administration of justice, II, 16—See Civil actions and procedure, Crimes and criminal procedure

Adults, person 18 years of age or older is adult for all purposes, II, 14

    person under 18 years of age entitled to all rights not specifically precluded, II, 15

Agriculture

    appropriations for protection, enhancement and development of agriculture, XII, 1

    department of agriculture, provision for, XII, 1

    levies on livestock and commodities for disease control and indemnification, predator control, inspection, protection, research and promotion, XII, 1

    maximum hours in regular day's work, agriculture and stock raising employment excepted, XII, 2

Amendment of constitution, XIV—See Constitution

Appeals

    district court jurisdiction, VII, 4

    procedural rules promulgated by supreme court, VII, 2

    supreme court jurisdiction, VII, 2

    tax appeals, VIII, 7

Appointments by governor

    department heads, **VI, 8**

    vacancy in executive office, VI, 6

Apportionment of state into legislative and congressional districts, procedure, V, 14

    accelerated effective date, Transition Schedule, Sec 1

Appropriations

    bills, generally, **V, 11**

    budget

        appropriations not to exceed anticipated revenue, VIII, 9

        governor to submit budget to legislature, VI, 9

    expenditures, strict accountability of state and local governmental entities, VIII, 12

        appropriation and issuance of warrant required, VIII, 14

Archaeologic areas, provision for preservation and administration, IX, 4

Armed forces—See Military affairs

Arms, right to bear, concealed weapons prohibited, II, 12

Arrests

    electors at polling places, immunity of, IV, 6

    legislative members, immunity of, V, 8

    warrant for arrest, requirements, II, 11

Assembly, freedom of, II, 6

Assessment of property for tax purposes, VIII, 3

Attainder of treason or felony by legislature prohibited, II, 30

Attorney general

    board of land commissioners, member of, X, 4

    candidacy for public office during term authorized, VI, 5

    compensation, **VI, 5**

        salary commission, creation, duties, XIII, 3

47

INDEX TO CONSTITUTION

References are Article and Section Numbers

Attorney general (Continued)

election, VI, 2
executive branch, member of, VI, 1
impeachment, subject to V, 13
legal officer of state, VI, 4
oath of office, III, 3
other government employment prohibited during term, VI, 5
qualifications, VI, 3
residence at seat of government, VI, 1
term of office, VI, 1
vacancy in office, how filled, VI, 6

Attorneys
bar admission, rules of supreme court, VII, 2
judicial officers, practice of law prohibited, VII, 9

Auditor
board of land commissioners, member of, X, 4
candidacy for public office during term authorized, VI, 5
compensation, VI, 5
  salary commission, creation, duties, XIII, 3
duties, VI 4
election, VI, 2
executive branch, member of, VI 1
impeachment, subject to, V, 13
oath of office, III, 3
other government employment prohibited during term VI, 5
qualifications, VI, 3
residence at seat of government, VI, 1
term of office, VI, 1
vacancy in office, how filled, VI, 6

B

Bail all but capital offenses bailable, II, 21
excessive bail prohibited, II, 22

Bar admission, rules of supreme court, VII, 2

Bear arms, right to, concealed weapons prohibited, II, 12

Bill of rights, II
procedural or substantive rights created for first time prospective and not retroactive, Transition Schedule, Sec 3
unenumerated rights not denied, impaired or disparaged, II, 34

Bills
adjournment of legislative session, pending bills carry over, V, 6
alteration or amendment changing original purpose prohibited, V, 11
appropriation bills, V, 11
ayes and noes to be recorded, V, 11
challenge of law for technical errors in passage time limit, V 11
private religious charitable, industrial, educational or benevolent purposes, appropriation for prohibited, V, 11
special or local acts prohibited, V, 12
subject clearly expressed in title V, 11
veto by governor, VI, 10
vote required for passage, V, 11

Board of land commissioners, X, 4

48

INDEX TO CONSTITUTION

49

INDEX TO CONSTITUTION

References are Article and Section Numbers

Civil rights, II
    education nondiscrimination in, X, 7
    procedural or substantive rights created for first time prospective and not retro-
        active, Transition Schedule, Sec 3
    unenumerated rights not denied, impaired or disparaged, II, 34
Code of ethics prohibiting conflicts of interest involving legislators and other public
    officials, XIII, 4
Colleges and universities, X—See Education
Commutations of sentences governor's power to grant, VI, 12
Compact with United States not affected by new constitution, I
Compensation of state officials
    judicial officers, VII, 7
        justices of the peace, VII, 5
    legislators, V, 6
    salary commission, creation, duties, XIII, 3
    state executive officers, VI, 5
Concealed weapons, carrying not permitted, II, 12
Conflicts of interest involving legislators and other public officials, code of ethics to be
    provided, XIII, 4
Congressional districts commission for redistricting and reapportioning the state, V, 14
    accelerated effective date Transition Schedule, Sec 1
Conservation
    environment, provision for protection and improvement, IX, 1
    reclamation of lands, IX, 2
    water rights, IX, 3
Constitution
    alteration or abolition of constitution as exclusive right of people, II, 2
    amendment
        convention, amendment by, XIV, 1 to 7—See constitutional convention, below
        initiative, amendment by, XIV, 9
            petition signers, XIV, 10
        more than one amendment submitted at same election, separate voting, XIV, 11
        other constitutional provisions on initiative or referendum not applicable, III, 8
    compact with United States not affected by new constitution, I
    constitutional convention, XIV, 1 to 7
        call of convention upon majority vote, XIV, 4
        delegates, number, qualifications, nomination, election, XIV, 4
            oath of delegates, XIV, 6
            vacancies, how filled, XIV, 6
        duties of convention, XIV, 7
        expenses of convention, XIV, 5
        initiative petition for convention, XIV, 2
            petition signers, XIV, 10
        meeting of convention, time fixed by legislature, XIV, 5
        other constitutional provisions on initiative or referendum not applicable, III, 8
        periodic submission to voters of question of holding convention, XIV, 3
        referendum on question of calling unlimited convention, vote required in legisla-
            ture, XIV, 1
        submission of revisions, alterations or amendments to voters, XIV, 7
    effective date, see note following Sec. 1 of Transition Schedule
        accelerated effective date of Art V, secs 6, 14, Transition Schedule, Sec 1
        delayed effective date of Art V, Secs. 1, 2, 3, Transition Schedule, Sec 2
    elective and appointive officers on effective date, terms of, Transition Schedule,
        Sec 6
    general transition, Transition Schedule, Sec 6

50

INDEX TO CONSTITUTION

Crimes and criminal procedure (Continued)
    information, criminal offenses prosecuted by, II, 20
    jury trial, right to, II, 26
        speedy public trial by impartial jury, II, 24
        unanimous verdict required, II, 26
    justice courts jurisdiction, VII, 5
    libel or slander, truth given in evidence, jury to determine law and facts, II, 7
    punishment founded on principles of prevention and reformation, II, 28
        cruel and unusual punishments prohibited II, 22
        restoration of rights on termination of state supervision, II 28
    rights of accused generally, II, 24
    searches and seizures, requirements for warrant, II, 11
    self incrimination, compulsion prohibited, II, 25
    speedy public trial, right to, II, 24
    supreme court jurisdiction, VII, 2
    venue of prosecutions, right to change, II, 24
    witnesses
        accused s right to meet face to face and have process to compel attendance II, 24
        detention of person as material witness, limitations on, II, 23

Cruel and unusual punishments prohibited, II, 22

Cultural resources, provision for preservation and administration IX, 4

D

Debt, imprisonment for prohibited, II, 27

Debt limitations
    balanced budget, VIII, 9
    local governmental entities establishment of limitations by legislature, VIII, 10
    state debt, VIII, 8

Decedents' estates, descent of, II, 30

Declaration of rights II
    procedural or substantive rights created for first time prospective and not retroactive, Transition Schedule Sec 3
    unenumerated rights not denied, impaired or disparaged, II, 34

Departments of state government
    agriculture department XII, 1
    appeals from administrative agencies, district court jurisdiction, VII, 4
    appointment of officers, VI, 8
    governor as supervisor of departments, VI, 8
    heads of departments, VI, 8
        removal from office is provided by law V, 11
        reports to governor, VI, 15
    labor and industry department, XII, 2
    number of principal departments, VI, 7
    single executive to head each department, VI, 8
    temporary commissions, VI, 7

Disabled persons, provision of economic assistance and social and rehabilitative services, XII 3

Disasters
    continuity of government, III 2
    governor's power to call militia forces, VI, 13
    importation of armed forces, application of legislature or governor, II, 33

52

Education (Continued)
  sectarian schools
    aid prohibited, exception, X, 6
    appropriation for private educational purposes prohibited, V, 11
  state board of education, composition, responsibilities, X, 9
  state s share of cost of elementary and secondary school system, X, 1
  superintendent of public instruction, VI, 1—See Superintendent of public instruction
  university funds, inviolate and guaranteed against loss or diversion, X, 10
    investment, VIII, 13; X, 10
  university system governed by board of regents, X, 9
    audit of funds under control of board, X, 9
    commissioner of higher education, appointment by board, X, 9
    governor ex officio member of board, X, 9
    superintendent of public instruction ex officio member of board, X, 9

Elections
  absentee voting requirements, IV, 3
  abuses of electoral process to be guarded against, IV, 3
  administration of elections, provision for, IV, 3
  arrest immunity at polling places, IV, 6
  ballot, secret ballot required, IV, 1
  candidates for public office, eligibility, IV, 4
  district court judges, selection, qualifications, VII, 8, 9
  electors, qualifications, IV, 2
  executive officers of state, terms, election, qualifications, VI, 1 to 3
  free exercise of suffrage guaranteed, II, 13
  immunity from arrest at polling places IV, 6
  justices of the peace, VII, 5
  largest number of votes elects, IV, 5
  legislators, election, terms and qualifications, V, 3, 4
    election and qualifications of members judged by each house, V, 10
  local government alternative form submitted to electors, XI, 9
    county government optional form, officers to be elected, XI, 3
    self-government charters, XI, 5
  poll booth registration authorized, IV, 3
  qualifications of electors, IV, 2
  registration requirements, IV, 3
  residence requirements, IV, 3
  results, largest number of votes elects, IV, 5
  secret ballot required, IV, 1
  supreme court justices, selection, qualifications, VII, 8, 9

Emergencies
  continuity of government, III, 2
  governor's authority to call militia forces, VI, 13
  importation of armed forces, application of legislature or governor, II, 33

Eminent domain, just compensation required, II, 29

Employment
  department of labor and industry, creation, appointment of commissioner, XII, 2
  injury incurred in employment, right to legal redress for, II, 16
  maximum hours in regular day's work, XII, 2
  pursuit of life's basic necessities, right to, II, 3

Enemy attack
  continuity of government, III, 2
  governor's authority to call militia forces, VI, 13
  importation of armed forces, application of legislature or governor, II, 33

Environment
  protection and improvement, IX, 1

H

I

J

L

References are Article and Section Numbers

References are Article and Section Numbers

64

Printed in the USA
CPSIA information can be obtained
at www.ICGtesting.com
LVHW010944060424
776640LV00011B/949